Lest We Forget: Lessons from Survivors of the Holocaust

Lest We Forget: Lessons from Survivors of the Holocaust

Debbie J. Callahan, M.S. Ed.

Published by Bruske Books Publishing House

Ocala, Florida

Books may be purchased by contacting the publisher at BruskeBooks@gmail.com or the author at: D.CallahanWritingServices @gmail.com. Discounts are available on bulk orders.

Cover Design: by Amanda Creek / Amanda Creek Creative.com

ISBN: 978-0-692-24284-1

Bruske Books Publishing House
Ocala, Florida

Table of Contents

Acknowledgements

For a book that I never intended to write, I received so much guidance and motivation that I had no choice but to write it and see it through to its completion. For this, I need to acknowledge several people. I wish to thank my mother Marianne Prescott and my husband Scott Sepper for always believing in me and my abilities as a writer, even at times when I doubted it myself. I need to thank my sons Matthew and Tyler Smith and Raynor Sepper and their lovely ladies for always encouraging me and treating me not only as a respected mother, but a cherished friend.

This book absolutely would not have been made without my dear friends and mentors parenting expert Bill Corbett and his wife Liz. Both are published authors and television hosts whom I so admire. No matter how many questions I barraged Bill with, he answered with wisdom and encouragement all the way through the process, and Liz became one of my biggest cheerleaders. Without my beautiful niece Amanda Creek of Amanda Creek Creative, I would not have the beautiful book cover you see before you, a book trailer, or even a website. She has gone above and beyond to bring beauty to my work, thus bringing it to life. Her wonderful husband David has also provided great inspiration to my efforts, and I appreciate all of them more than I can adequately express.

Additionally, I wish to recognize the Holocaust Memorial Education and Resource Center of Maitland, Florida, and some of its wonderful employees for conducting an amazing Teachers Institute for Holocaust Studies each year that is life-changing, educating the public on a wide variety of human rights issues, and for allowing me to be a small part of their team as a volunteer. The center has helped me decide to make the Holocaust and its lessons the focus of my writing. Through them, I was able to form relationships with some of the survivors that have influenced this writing, and has led to my special friendship with one in particular, Helen Greenspun, my hero.

Finally, I want to give my heartfelt thanks to Rabbi Ephraim Rubinger and his wonderful wife Ruchama Rubinger who have helped me as my soul has found its way home. They have taught me so much about Judaism, which has helped me form stronger bonds to some of my own roots and to understand those whose stories I share at a much deeper level.

There are many others to thank, proofreaders, friends, coworkers, family, and the readers of my article. Their overwhelming response led to the idea to create the books. I am so blessed for each and every one of you. ~ Debbie

Fragments of Indifference

Far in the distance, a train whistle pierces the silence of twilight
Conjuring romantic visions of far- off exotic destinations
Visualizing tired passengers lulled to slumber by a gentle rocking
Wheels gliding along the well-traveled steel
Occupants catching glimpses of water below as
The train precariously navigates a narrow bridge
Persistent barking of a protective dog protesting an impressive trespasser
For some perhaps a journey home, for others, a break away
Where will it light?
What weary, yet exuberant travelers will finally settle there?

Then the screams… the crying
Protective barking now incessant canine growling
Brutal shouts in German and English, "Raus! Raus! Out! Out!"
Upon rousing from my dreamlike state, I realize…
It is another one of THOSE trains.

Will it never end? Won't anyone stop this madness?
Covering my head with my pillow, I attempt to shut out the now familiar sounds… and the smell.
The train ride for some a journey home, for others a break away, for millions during the Holocaust….a trip to Hell that no one stopped

-Indifference

Leaving incomplete lives…only fragments of what was once humanity
~Debbie Callahan (2014)

Introduction

First-hand witnesses to one of the worst events in recent history will soon be a thing of the past. With many Holocaust survivors passing away each day, it won't be long before we must rely on textbooks and second-generation testimony to learn of the atrocities that they experienced during the reign of Adolf Hitler and the Nazi party. For a while longer, though, we still have this valuable resource, and many of them continue to share their stories with one audience after another, despite the pain of reliving the horrific events that we cannot even begin to imagine.

One might wonder not only how they are able to retell these details day after day, but more importantly, why? Most will tell you that they do this to disprove the deniers and to be the voice of their friends and loved ones who did not survive to speak for themselves. Some of their messages are unexpected, while others leave a strong impact on the recipient. All of them, though, should be heeded.

This book is in part the result of befriending an amazing woman. As an 87 year-young Holocaust survivor, her strength, grace, and amazing testimony instantly provided me with a hero and role model. Hearing of her capture as a 15 year-old girl in Poland is hard enough to handle, but when she talks of her starvation, her whippings as a result of trying to sneak food, and the Treblinka gassing of her younger brother, sister, and parents, it is absolutely heart-wrenching. Thankfully, she had four other siblings with her during most of her two labor camp and five concentration camp incarceration spanning over three-and-a-half years (followed by four years in a displaced person camp).

When asked why she continues to share her painful story over and over again to large groups of students and others, she makes it clear that there were many girls left behind to die during a death march that she survived. She speaks for them as she still remembers them lying there, too weak to move on, and waving their arms, calling to be helped. Yet, Helen and the others would have been shot by the Nazis had they tried to help their friends, former schoolmates, even family members. It is for them that she speaks and relives the horrors that consumed far too large a portion of her life.

Having heard Helen deliver this message to hundreds of students and teachers over the past three years has taught me about humility, courage, strength, and the importance of keeping history alive for future generations. Becoming her friend has absolutely changed my life. For these reasons, I have promised her, and every other survivor I have met, that I will devote a large portion of my own life to keeping their stories alive, so future generations do not have to learn about them from a simple paragraph in a textbook. I will also share these stories to assure that everyone understands these horrific events did happen, regardless of how they may get watered down with the passing of time. The following includes messages from some of the survivors I have met, and many others who concur, that they feel you must keep their messages alive.

Author Debbie Callahan
and
Survivor Helen Garfinkel-Greenspun
2013

Chapter 1

The Holocaust and its Survivors

Although this book is not intended as a complete history of the Holocaust and is written based on my own study and research of the events included within those crucial years of 1933-1945, it is important that we begin with a concise definition of what the Holocaust was. Yad Vashem World Center for Holocaust Research, Documentation, Education and Commemoration in Israel defines the Holocaust as:

> The sum total of all anti-Jewish actions carried out by the Nazi regime between 1933 and 1945: from stripping the German Jews of their legal and economic status in the 1930s`; segregating and starvation in the various occupied countries; the murder of close to six million Jews in Europe. (The holocaust: Definition, 2014)

However, the term Holocaust was not used until the 1950s. As early as the 1940s, the term Shoah (a Hebrew word) was used to describe the destruction of European Jewry. Both words may be used within the text to follow, which is, in fact, intended as a means of expressing important lessons from the events survived by extraordinary people.

While most of the first-hand testimonies on which I base the lessons in this book do come from Jewish survivors, Jews were not the only victims of the Shoah. I must also point out that close to five million non-

Jews, including Jehovah Witnesses, homosexuals, Gypsies, the disabled, and others, perished at the hands of the Nazis as well. An estimated eleven million lives taken, but there are many other victims who survived.

The fact that anyone survived such complete annihilation is truly miraculous. If one stops to consider the number of casualties by country, the low odds of survival are clearly seen. Poland, for example, according to the Jewish Virtual Library, lost 90% of its Jewish population; yet, I have the privilege of knowing a few Holocaust survivors from Poland. (Holocaust Denial, 2001) I consider their presence in my life a miracle and a gift that I will treasure forever, and each of their stories of survival vastly differs from one another.

One source of survival came from courageous non-Jewish individuals and families who hid Jews. These brave souls put their own lives at risk with the full knowledge that they would suffer the same fate as those Jews who were rapidly disappearing at the hands of the Nazis. Often hidden by Christian families, many Jews managed to survive the war, despite Adolf Hitler's best efforts to eradicate all of European Jewry.

Other Jewish children were spared via passage on Kinder Transports. Parents were forced to make gut-wrenching decisions to place their children on these transports, knowing that the chance of ever surviving to see them again were slim. Yet, parents made this sacrifice, and as a result, thousands of children survived by leaving Nazi-held territories for the safety of Great Britain. These means of survival will be further discussed later in this book as I begin to share messages of those who lived through the Shoah and lessons about the dangerous actions and attitudes that led to it.

While there were many other forms of survival as well, some of the most memorable accounts come from those who survived despite actually spending time in the camps. Against all odds, these heroes endured humiliation, freezing temperatures, beatings, torture, hard labor, lice, and disease. They lived, or perhaps existed might be a better word, surrounded by death. By the time they were liberated, those who could still walk resembled the walking dead themselves. In addition to the deplorable conditions in which they had to suffer within the labor, concentration, or extermination camps, thousands were forced on death marches.

The United States Holocaust Memorial Museum describes death marches as follows:

> Prisoners were forced to march long distances in bitter cold, with little or no food, water, or rest. Those who could not keep up were shot. The largest death marches took place in the winter of 1944-1945, when the Soviet army began its liberation of Poland. Nine days before the Soviets arrived at Auschwitz, the Germans marched tens of thousands of prisoners out of the camp toward Wodzislaw, a town thirty-five miles away, where they were put on freight trains to other camps. About one in four died on the way. (The Holocaust Memorial Museum, 2013)

Imagining what such a march would have been like is difficult for any of us, but at the time of this writing in the year 2014, we still have survivors among us who were there and who are willing to share stories of those harrowing walks. Holocaust survivors want you to know the horrible situations they went through. They also want everyone to realize that not only was it possible for such things to take place, but that they DID take place, and to never forget that they did. Most importantly, they want you to keep their stories alive long after they are gone, so that there is never any doubt about these facts.

Death march from Dachau photo: United States Holocaust Memorial Museum, Washington, DC

Chapter 2
Denying the Holocaust

With the passing of time, memories of events in history tend to fade. Some become more unbelievable as the years sweep farther from events that were once incredibly real and frightening. In any episode in history, our most valuable resources come in the form of first-hand testimony. Whether verbal or written, nothing can compare to direct information from people who lived through times that many of the generations since cannot even begin to imagine.

Fortunately, many of these survivors, rescuers, and liberators continue to tell their stories. Well, into their 80s and 90s at the time of this writing, World War II witnesses tirelessly relive their experiences, regardless of the pain it inflicts upon them, to educate us and future generations about the atrocities they witnessed or suffered. Yet, these very people, who lay their hearts and souls on the line each and every time they accept a speaking engagement, must chance confronting deniers.

Sometimes in the form of aggressive protestors, and other times, it might simply be one opinionated teenager in a school audience, but even that one student verbally attacking a survivor can cause a great deal of pain. How can one voice have such an effect? It's simple. They insist one of two points, either that the Holocaust never happened, or that it was greatly exaggerated by the Jews and the press for various reasons. Abraham H. Foxman, National Director of the Anti-Defamation League, comments that, Iranian "President Mahmoud Ahmadinejad, among others, suggested that Jews control sources of information and created the so-called 'fantasy' of the Holocaust to win support for Israel." (Foxman, 2007)

To you or me, Ahmadinejad's insults and accusations may not seem like all of that much of a threat. After all, it is just the opinion of one person, or one small group of people. Yet, these episodes are not nearly as harmless as they sound. As the president of Iran, one can only assume that Ahmadinejad would have had influence over at least some of the people who voted him into office. When such a powerful public figure not only holds, but also openly vocalizes such views, the toxicity has the potential of spreading at lightning speed. It behooves us to remember another powerful leader who held Anti-Semitic views, and recall where his ideas led, namely, Adolf Hitler.

Let's also consider the impact on the survivors. Losing family members in any manner is difficult. Knowing that they were intentionally murdered or starved to death because of their religion, age, or health, is almost impossible to accept. Yet, they somehow garner the strength to go on and continue living, only to be told years later that it never happened, unfathomable. I can't imagine the feelings of pain and anger that would incite, and the unfairness of it for those who survived the atrocities of the Shoah is reprehensible.

Also of concern is the naivety of today's youth and how blindly some tend to follow others. As I read and watch news stories about it, I am surprised that even with laws in place in some countries concerning Holocaust denial and with documentation more readily available than ever before, that it is even possible for anyone to deny that it happened. Proof is right at people's fingertips, thanks to the Internet and websites for places such as the United States Holocaust Memorial Museum and Yad Vashem in Israel; yet, there are still deniers of the Holocaust and people categorized by the more recent term, "Holocaust Revisionists."

Let's take a look at what they are saying. According to the Anti-Defamation League, Robert Faurisson stated the following in The Guardian Weekly on April 7, 1991:

> The alleged Hitlerian gas chambers and the alleged genocide of the Jews form one and the same historical lie, which permitted a gigantic financial swindle whose chief beneficiaries have been the State of Israel and international Zionism, and whose main victims have been the German people and the Palestinian people as a whole. (Representative Quotes, 2001)

Then of course, there is the quite well-known David Irving, who according to the Anti-Defamation League stated the following in Speech in Portland, Oregon on September 18, 1996.

> "When I get to Australia in January I know what is going to happen. They are going to wheel out all the so-called eyewitnesses. One in particular, Mrs. Altman, I've clashed with once or twice. She is very

convincing. They can be very convincing because they have to do it so often over the years. They've had a free run. We're going to meet because she has that tattoo. I am going to say, 'You have that tattoo, we all have the utmost sympathy for you. But how much money have you made on it! In the last 45 years! Can I estimate! Quarter of a million! Half million! Certainly not less. That's how much you've made from the German taxpayers and the American taxpayers.' Ladies and gentlemen, you're paying $3 billion a year to the State of Israel. Compensation to people like Mrs. Altman. She'll say, 'Why not, I suffered.' I'll say you didn't. You survived. By definition you didn't suffer. Not half as much as those who died.... They suffered. You didn't. You're the one making the money. Explain to me this. Why have you people made all the money, but Australian soldiers who suffered for five years in Japanese prison camps haven't got a bent nickel out of it!" (Representative Quotes, 2001)

Some common messages deniers use to build their cases are as follows:

1. The Holocaust Did Not Occur Because There Is No Single "Master Plan" for Jewish Annihilation

2. There Were No Gas Chambers Used for Mass Murder at Auschwitz and Other Camps

3. Holocaust Scholars Rely on the Testimony of Survivors Because There Is No Objective Documentation Proving the Nazi Genocide

4. There Was No Net Loss of Jewish Lives Between 1941 and 1945

5. The Nuremberg Trials Were a "Farce of Justice" Staged for the Benefit of the Jews (Jewish Virtual Library)

Part of the "evidence" they use to support their denial of the gassing of people is the use of Zyklon B. They explain that there is a blue residue or staining that results in any building where it was used (for delousing, according to these deniers), and they try to prove that places such as Treblinka were not extermination camps, but rather transit camps. Their proof? The lack of blue staining. They neglect to mention that it was not the only method of gassing. For example, Treblinka used Carbon Monoxide gas and diesel engines for their gassings, which does not leave blue stains.

Holocaust survivors want you to know that these are all blatant lies that are spread to convince the modern world that what they lived through was not real or was at least exaggerated. They want you to dispute the claims of deniers, so our future generations do not grow up believing such grotesque fallacies. They must know the truth, or we open the door to possible similar reoccurrences.

Why or how can anyone deny the Holocaust or downplay the tragedies it caused during its existence? Admittedly, the idea that at least 6 million Jews and 5 million others were systematically killed under the leadership of the Nazi government is quite inconceivable. For those too young to have experienced World War II first-hand and hear daily stories on the radio or seeing newsreels at the cinema, the events can seem unreal and fantastically fabricated when one first hears of them. After all, if Jews and others were being conscripted, mistreated, starved, and killed at the hands of the Nazi government, why didn't anyone try to stop them? They couldn't have been allowed to continue such genocide.

Auschwitz Photo Credit: Simon Bell

Also, the question arises of why Jews didn't just leave at the first sign of a threat, or why didn't they fight back? So yes, at first encounter, it might be seen as a myth, but the average person with an open mind listens and learns. Uncovering the truth doesn't require much digging. Unfortunately today, not everyone takes the time to develop a healthy curiosity and furthermore, search for answers. People may listen to falsehoods; accept them without digging any deeper for the truth.

When considering our younger generations, think of how they are so far removed from the events of our past, and realize that they have little connection to anything that happened before their own time, and that leaves them vulnerable for influence from potentially unreliable sources. With most not growing up with the benefit of nightly dinner table discussions about the events of World War II, and quite honestly, many do not have the benefit of dinner table conversations at all any longer, the link to the Holocaust is just not there, especially in non-Jewish families. So where do these people turn for the facts as they discover the Holocaust for the first time? Well, there is always school reading, often mere impersonal paragraphs in textbooks, but usually the first place one will turn to is the Internet.

While it is an incredibly valuable tool, and one that I myself wonder how I ever lived without, it can also be dangerous to naive, trusting youth. We can begin by looking at one of the first options at the top of almost every search list, Wikipedia. Although it can be a reliable source that is effective in providing links to other resources, the content is not always one hundred percent correct. Not only is it written by people who are not necessarily experts, but people can, and do, change the content, perhaps making it inaccurate and sometimes comical. For example, in 2012, as I was teaching a lesson about the Holocaust and the reliability of resources to my middle school students, I randomly did an Internet search on World War II. The first choice on the search list was Wikipedia. I clicked on it, not having checked it in advance, and I could not have chosen a better example if I had researched it for days.

The example I selected began with an introduction to the events that led to the war, even going into detail about the beginnings in both Europe and the Pacific. Part way through paragraph two or three, in the middle of a sentence about aircraft carriers the phrase "sometimes my poo turns green" was inserted, and the aircraft carrier sentence continued on as professionally as it had begun. While you can probably imagine the delight this brought to a class full of thirteen year-old students, it did also teach a serious lesson. These sites are not always reliable and are not to be trusted alone. It is not my intent to stop people from using Wikipedia, but people must search more than one resource, something most teens will not naturally do.

Additionally, when these young people search the Internet, they discover not only facts, but the opinions of many others. Some of these will be deniers or revisionists writing about "The Holocaust Hoax." These can be convincing, and at times sneaky. I have even been fooled, albeit briefly, by some of these sites, one of which led me to a documentary about Adolf Hitler. I confess I am a sucker for a documentary; I love them and watch them daily. Therefore, I began to watch this one. Soon enough though, its intent clearly surfaced, and I knew that it was a very well-done show meant to glorify Hitler and justify his actions. Professionally done, this film could easily get the attention of, and convincingly persuade, an uninformed person that Hitler was the victim of his circumstances and not the monster that people portray him to be, a dangerous misconception.

The techniques used by the deniers are not that different from the propaganda tactics of the Nazis themselves. Furthermore, there is another disturbing similarity; the people spreading these lies are not doing so out of ignorance. Many are quite educated, holding graduate degrees and working as professors, doctors, or in other reputable career fields. Yet, they deny the evidence and downplay those events that are recorded. Then they spread their lies or misconceptions.

According to the United States Holocaust Memorial Museum, these deniers claim that the Jews needed "the myth" of the Holocaust so they could get compensation from Germany and to further their cause for an independent state of Israel. Additionally, they propose that the Allies (America, Great Britain, France, and the Soviet Union at varying times) created this myth to justify their occupation of Germany and the persecution of war criminals. (Holocaust Deniers, 2013)

Deniers insist that in the absence of one succinct order directly from Hitler that outlines the Holocaust, it must not have happened. With a firm conviction that it was a hoax, they ignore the evidence that is available, records actually kept by the Germans. They pass them off as forgeries and continue to distort facts to suit their claims. Beyond the paperwork deniers choose to overlook, there is denial on a larger scale such as the existence of gas chambers, which they say were simply delousing chambers or morgues, totally disregarding once again the fact that Nazi records clearly show otherwise. As for the limited physical evidence available, they neglect to consider the fact that the Nazis did everything within their power to destroy such evidence as they retreated under threat of the Allied forces. (Holocaust deniers, 2013) Fortunately, they were not completely successful as evidenced at Majdanek and Auschwitz in Poland.

Why do these people deny the Holocaust? With some remaining structures open for visitation, glaring detailed Nazi documentation, and most commanding of all, Holocaust survivors willing to share their testimony, how is it possible that intelligent and well-read professional people can refute such evidence? Yet, the American chief prosecutor

Robert Jackson foresaw it happening and stated during the Nuremberg Trials, "Unless record is made … future generations would not believe how horrible the truth was." (Evidence from, 2013) He was correct, because denial does exist, and with our young people who are easily led astray and quick to believe the first thing they read, the danger of the disbelief or watering down of the events of the Holocaust is all too real.

Holocaust survivors want you to know that these events did indeed happen, and they have not been in any way exaggerated. Don't let the passage of time diminish the memories of what was, and don't ever forget. The evidence is there. Even though Rudolf Höess, former commander of Auschwitz, admitted that records were not kept of all of those victims who were chosen for immediate killing, he provides proof that it did happen. Below, partial testimony from Höess during the Nuremberg trials demonstrates all too clearly the gravity of the selection process used to determine the fate of millions.

Nuremberg Trials – testimony of Rudolf Höess

BY DR. KAUFFMANN:

Q. From 1940 to 1943, you were the commandant of the camp at Auschwitz. Is that true?

A. Yes.

Q. And during that time, hundreds of thousands of human beings were sent to their death there, Is that correct?

A. Yes.

Q. Is it true that you, yourself, have made no exact notes regarding the figures of the number of those victims because you were forbidden to make them?

A. Yes, that is correct.

Q. Is it furthermore correct that only one man, by the name of Eichmann, recorded the figures, the man who had the task of organising and assembling these people?

A. Yes.

Q. Is it furthermore true that Eichmann stated to you that in Auschwitz a sum total of more than two million Jews had been destroyed?

A. Yes.

Q. Men, women and children?

A. Yes.

Then further on in the testimony, he continues with the following:

Q. And after the arrival of the transports did the victims have to dispose of everything they had? Did they have to undress completely; did they have to surrender their valuables? Is that true?

A. Yes.

Q. And then they immediately went to their death?

A. Yes.

Q. I ask you, according to your knowledge, did these people know what was in store for them?

A. The majority of them did not, for steps were taken to keep them in doubt about it so that the suspicion would not arise that they were to go to their death. For instance, all doors and all walls bore inscriptions to the effect that they were going to undergo a delousing operation or take a shower. This was proclaimed in several languages to the detainees by other detainees who had come in with earlier transports and who were being used as auxiliary crews during the whole action.

Q. And then, you told me the other day, that death from gassing occurred within a period of three to fifteen minutes. Is that correct?

A. Yes.

Q. You also told me that even before death definitely set in the victims fell into a state of unconsciousness?

A. Yes. From what I was able to find out myself or from what was told me by medical officers, the time necessary for the arrival of unconsciousness or death varied according to the temperature and the number of people present in the chambers. Loss of consciousness took place after a few seconds or minutes. (UMKC)

The defendants and their lawyers at the International Military Tribunal Trial of war criminals at Nuremberg. Photograph: #61323 Credits: National Archives and Records Administration, College Park- Copyright: Public Domain

If perhaps you feel that one man's word is not enough, Nazi documents exist referring to gas tight doors, rubberized sealing strips, and inspection peepholes. (Myers, 2009) More incriminating still is the fact that the former commandant of Auschwitz-Birkenau, Höess, even signed the following affidavit in May of 1946 as explained in Auschwitz Scrapbook on Scrapbookpages.com. The English translation of the German text in the affidavit reads:

"I declare herewith under oath that in the years 1941 to 1943 during my tenure in office as commandant of Auschwitz Concentration Camp 2 million Jews were put to death by gassing and a 1/2 million by other means. Rudolf Höess. May 14, 1946." The confession was signed by

Höess and by Josef Maier of the US Chief of Counsel's office. (Scrapbook, 2005) So with this admission of gassing at Auschwitz by the camp commander, does that sound like the "gas" chambers were used solely for "delousing purposes" as deniers and revisionists claim? This evidence is not enough to convince deniers and revisionists though. They contend that Höess was forced into making the statements that he did.

Höess is not the only former camp resident to admit to the nature of operations at Auschwitz. Oskar Gröning began as a bookkeeper of sorts, hand-selected, to keep track of the money stolen from the new arrivals on the transports. He was later put in charge of guarding the luggage and valuables. Although he carries no guilt, he feels that what happened at Auschwitz was part of warfare. He was also quite disturbed by some of the atrocities that he witnessed there. He has been haunted by them for years, and after all of this time, still loses sleep and hears the victims' screams. After many years, he decided to speak out. In the Public Broadcasting System's *Auschwitz: Inside the Nazi State*, he states the following:

> "I see it as my task, now at my age, to face up to these things that I experienced and to oppose the Holocaust deniers who claim that Auschwitz never happened. And that's why I am here today. Because I want to tell those deniers: I have seen the gas chambers, I have seen the crematoria, I have seen the burning pits - and I want you to believe me that these atrocities happened. I was there." (Public Broadcast System & Laurence Rees. 2005)

In another interview, he reiterates what he said above, and adds a bit more:

> "I would like you to believe me," he says. "I saw the gas chambers. I saw the crematorium. I saw the open fires. I was on the ramp when the selections took place. I would like you to believe that these atrocities happened, because I was there." (Shofar FTP Archives)

Coincidently, in the year of this publication 2014, 93-year-old Gröning will finally face trial as he has finally been charged with 300,000 counts of accessory to murder.

We should also consider the testimony of surviving members of the Sonderkommando units. These were the inmates who were hand-selected, often as they arrived on the transport, to do the dirty work of the camp. They were the people who had to go into the gas chambers that deniers say were used for delousing and pull out the bodies to either bury them or take them to the crematoria to burn them. Surviving members of a Sonderkommando are rare. Generally, they too were killed in the gas chambers, possibly as early as at the end of the day, but usually after a few weeks to several months of work.

Of those who did survive, some have since passed away of old age or health issues. As people who experienced the worst of the worst, they were sometimes charged with getting the Jews into the undressing rooms and into the gas chambers. Often these were the same people who came in on the same transport as the Sonderkommando, and might even have been related to him. The psychological impact of being forced to lead friends, loved ones, or even strangers to their death was something they could never come to terms with in their lifetimes.

To be a bit more specific about the tasks with which the members of these units were charged, I include the following:

> The Sonderkommando were Jewish prisoners who worked the death camps in return for special treatment and privileges. Every few months, the current group was liquidated and the first task of their successors was to dispose of the bodies of the previous group. Since a Sonderkommando was usually comprised of men from incoming transports, their second task often consisted of disposing of the bodies of their own families.
>
> The Sonderkommando did not participate directly in the actual killing — that was carried out by the Nazis. The Sonderkommando duties included guiding the new arrivals into the gas chambers, removing the bodies afterwards, shaving hair, removing teeth, sorting through possessions (much of which they were given as reward), cremating the bodies, and disposing of the ashes. Their knowledge of the internal workings of the camp marked them for certain death. Someone selected for the Sonderkommando had a choice: die then or die in four months time. During the summer of 1944, thousands of new Jewish prisoners were arriving at the death camp by the day— especially from Hungary. The increase of prisoners necessitated the enlargement of the Sonderkommando. (Pappas, 2014)

Considering one of the biggest arguments of the deniers is that no one ever saw someone get killed in a gas chamber, I submit this to show that yes, there were witnesses. Members of the Sonderkommando saw it all too closely. Unfortunately, some could never come to terms with the atrocities that they had seen and been forced to participate in, and they ended up taking their own lives, some by throwing themselves against the electrified fence, and others, years later.

Individual records exist of Holocaust victims as well. Yad Vashem and the United States Holocaust Memorial Museum maintain excellent data bases to find information on many of the people who survived, hid, or perished during the Holocaust. Armed with such information, fighting denial or claims of revisionists becomes a little easier.

Photograph:#61985Credit: National Archives and Records Administration, College Park Beit Lohamei Haghetaot (Ghetto Fighters' House Museum) Ministere des Anciens Combattants et Victimes de Guerre. Copyright: Public Domain

After having taught about the Holocaust for several years, I discovered an unknown connection to one branch of a Jewish family from which I am descended. This was an amazing discovery, since I was raised surrounded by Irish Catholic family members. I had no experience with Jewish people at all and didn't realize there was a connection in my own family until much later. The discovery that I am in part descended from Ashkenazi Jews of Amsterdam led to much research and revelation, not all of it good. My distant family in Amsterdam, relatives on my maternal grandfather's side, was nearly annihilated by the Nazis. With nearly two hundred members (and the number climbs as I continue my research) killed during the Holocaust, the fact that I exist at all is truly a miracle. The discovery of my personal connection to the Shoah will soon be detailed in my next book following the completion of further research planned at Auschwitz in January of 2015.

As I have researched the records of these distant relatives, finding exact dates and locations of their demise, I've discovered that most of them died in Sobibor and Auschwitz. During this research, I came across a blog article with a letter addressed to tie Iranian Embassy concerning President Ahmadinejad of Iran that speaks of some of these distant family members. Daniel Teeboom's letter sums up the ridiculousness of the president's denial perfectly. In it, he expresses that since the president of a country says the Holocaust never happened, it must be so, therefore, he expects the immediate return of several family members, in which he includes an extensive list of names with their places and dates of death. I can't help but appreciate the sarcasm. Yet, ignoring the gravity of the tragedy of the family deaths contained within it is impossible. (Teeboom, 2005)

Auschwitz survivor, Primo Levi, once said, "If the world could become convinced that Auschwitz never existed, it would be easier to build a second Auschwitz, and there is no assurance it would devour only Jews" (Sheehan, 2001. P.59) The fact that evidence does exist and fortunately, for the time being, so do some eye witnesses, should stop any form of denial or revisionism, but clearly it is not enough. All of those resources are of no use if people are not led to them, or if we who know, do not spread those messages and vocalize these truths.

Doing so is not a matter of glamorizing a horrific event, nor is it an attempt to remain martyrs or dwell in victim mentality. Keeping these messages alive and continuing to speak of them regardless of the passing years educates each generation in an effort to prevent history from repeating itself. Out of respect for those who lived through the Holocaust and for the preservation of a more humane future, tell these stories and lead others to the evidence. Only through these means can we hope the term "Never Again!" can become a reality in which we can all securely believe.

Survivors of the Holocaust want you to realize how large of a problem denial is. Whether someone denies that it happened at all or only denies certain events or killing methods, the messages can be detrimental to the truth of history and the education of vulnerable and naive youth in this and the generations to come. Survivors want you to fight denial wherever you see it and in whatever form it exists.

Chapter Three

Distorting the Numbers

Closely related to Holocaust denial is "Distortion," often used by revisionists. According to the Government of Canada, where many survivors settled after liberation, Holocaust Distortion can be defined as the following:

1. Intentional efforts to excuse or minimize the impact of the Holocaust or its principal elements, including collaborators and allies of Nazi Germany;

2. Gross minimization of the number of the victims of the Holocaust in contradiction to reliable sources;

3. Attempts to blame the Jews for causing their own genocide;

4. Statements that cast the Holocaust as a positive historical event. Those statements are not Holocaust denial but are closely connected to it as a radical form of anti-Semitism. They may suggest that the Holocaust did not go far enough in accomplishing its goal of "the Final Solution of the Jewish Question";

5. Attempts to blur the responsibility for the establishment of concentration and death camps devised and operated by Nazi

> Germany by putting blame on other nations or ethnic groups. (Backgrounder — working, 2013)

When it comes to minimizing the number of victims, I have to wonder why. What purpose does it serve? Any and every person left to starve to death, die of diseases and harsh, unsanitary conditions, executed or gassed, is one senseless death too many. These vicious acts of inhumanity are no less heinous if by chance fewer victims may have died than estimated. Yet, Holocaust survivors want you to know that the number of deaths is NOT exaggerated. If anything, it may be understated.

Achieving a complete and accurate count of victims is impossible; however, "Research by some of the world's most able historians places the number of Holocaust victims murdered by German government policy to be not less than twelve million and probably more." (Gilbert, 1993) Attaining an exact number is difficult for a few reasons. First of all, many infants were killed without their births ever having been registered anywhere. Since often the counts are done using pre and post-war census data, certainly there would be discrepancies where non-registered births are involved.

There are also deaths that may not be recorded. Steven Morse and Peter Landé point out in *Introduction to Dachau Concentration Camp Records*,

> "It must be acknowledged that millions of persons who perished will never be identified and/or their fate known. This is particularly true of East European Jews who were rarely taken to camps where

records were maintained but rather were murdered where they resided or taken to extermination camps which did not maintain such records." (Morse & Lande', 2008)

Of the recorded number of deaths, it is hard to determine if deaths such as suicides are accounted for accurately. Following the Nazis' rise to power in 1933, many Jews in despair took their own lives as a result of the violent treatment imposed upon them. Great numbers of suicides occurred during large actions such as Kristallnacht, also known as "Crystal Night" or the "Night of Broken Glass," which was a large government sanctioned pogrom against Jewish homes, businesses, synagogues.

In just one night in November of 1938, according to the United States Holocaust Memorial Museum, over 267 synagogues were destroyed, and "SA and Hitler Youth members across the country shattered the shop windows of an estimated 7,500 Jewish-owned commercial establishments, and looted their wares. Jewish cemeteries became a particular object of desecration in many regions." (Kristallnacht: A nationwide, 2013) All of these actions were devastating to the Jews, but the violence didn't end there. Many were beaten, raped, incarcerated, killed, and yes, some committed suicide.

Suicides continued to mount in the years that followed as the Jews were systematically forced out of their jobs and as their businesses were boycotted and later transferred into Nazi hands. Between the humiliation and the financial desperation, many Jews chose to end their lives.

In some instances, these self-inflicted deaths were a way to avoid capture and deportation. Some were the result of fear or hopelessness, and others were a form of resistance, but since so many of these deaths happened early and not in the camps, ascertaining if all of them were recorded in the statistics of the "killings" is not easy to determine with certainty. Yet, it is important to recognize them because all were senseless, and all were a direct result of Hitler's rise to power.

SS troops stand near the bodies of Jews who committed suicide by jumping from a fourth story window rather than be captured during the suppression of the Warsaw Ghetto uprising. The original German caption reads: "Bandits who jumped."

There were also suicides in the camps. According to Tamara Traubmann, a correspondent for *Haaretz*, "Recent studies found that while 100 suicides per 100,000 people is considered a very high rate in normal times, the rate in the camps was about 25,000 suicides per 100,000 people, or almost one out of every four people." (Traubman, 2005) The most common method of suicide for camp inmates was throwing themselves against the electrically charged wire fences that surrounded the camps.

Are the numbers exaggerated? Does it really matter? If there were fewer deaths than recorded, does it make the tragedy any less real? Does it lessen the despair, pain, and terror of the victims? Absolutely not! No one can realistically water down the effects of the Holocaust. We may never have exact numbers, but if we stop to think about the many ways people were killed or died from 1933-1945, it is not unrealistic to assume that there were many deaths which were not accounted for in Holocaust statistics.

If we really want to get technical with the number of deaths, we might even consider the number of births prevented as a result of the forced sterilizations enforced by the Nazis, but we can never really put a number on the amount of future teachers, doctors, writers, mothers, or artists that might have been. How many musicians or leaders may have been born had the chance been given? Then, we might consider the children and grandchildren that will never be. Of course those numbers would stretch long beyond World War II, so they couldn't be counted, but we must still remember that family lines were cut short.

Holocaust-related deaths continued beyond the war as well. In the displaced persons camps that housed many survivors for the years following liberation and the end of the war, news filtered in, and adjustments had to be made. People had to find a way back to the land of the living after being surrounded for so long by death. After having lived every moment watching and fearing death, they had to once again learn how to live. They also, in many cases, had to find something to live for after so much loss.

It was during this time when survivors had nowhere else to go, that they were cared for in camps set up by the Allied Forces and the UNRRA (United Nations Relief and Rehabilitation Administration) (USHMM). Here they were clothed, fed, and educated, but here they were also informed. This temporary home is where many learned the outcome of their homes, and more importantly, the fate of their family members from whom they had been separated. The news was not often good.

With no home to return to, and often, no surviving family, how does one find a reason to go on? Doing so, took almost as much courage as surviving the concentration camps.

It was in one such camp, where a friend of mine lived for four years following her three-and-a-half year captivity. In this DP camp in Germany, she learned of the destruction of her village and the Treblinka gassing of her parents, seven year-old brother, and nine-year-old sister. Ironically, she credits her survival of the camps and death marches to staying alive for her mother's sake. She tells me that she worried so much that her mother would cry and be so upset if her children died. She never knew that her mother and other family members were killed within a few weeks of her capture. Fortunately, she had three sisters and a brother who survived the camps with her, and they leaned heavily on one another. Not everyone was as fortunate, though.

Too many people found themselves to be the lone survivor of an entire family. Some had the strength to move on with their lives. Others, did not, and took their own lives right there in the DP camps. Many rushed ahead trying to build new lives and families. New couples united in marriage, and life began anew. In one such camp, there were 200 women pregnant at the same time within 15 months of its opening. (Wortman, et. al. p.5) After leaving the DP camps, these couples found new homes in new lands, many landing in Canada or eventually, Israel. Others created lives in the United States. We will revisit the DP camp and immigration experiences in upcoming chapters; however, for now, know that all was not blissful.

Rebuilding in the shadow of so much loss, grief, and amongst the ghosts of the past, was certainly not easy. As a result, regardless of the number of years that pass, studies show that Holocaust survivors are three times more likely to commit suicide in their old age than those who did not experience the effects of the Holocaust.

A 2005 *JWeekly.com* article titled "Study: Trauma of Holocaust triples survivors' suicide risk" discussed a study done for the "American Journal of Geriatric Psychiatry," Professor Yoram Barak looked at the medical records of patients for the previous five years. He found that they showed of the 374 Holocaust survivors who were inpatients, that 90 had attempted suicide, but of the 502 patients who had not been through the

Holocaust, only 45 had attempted suicide. Not all of the attempts made by survivors ended there; some were successful. (Study: Trauma of, 2005)

If we factor in these losses, I contend the number of Jews killed is not at all exaggerated. If anything, it is low and should include these more recent casualties as well. For the sake of the survivors, if we hear of this tragic event being down-played, we must remember each victim as a human, and one who was connected to a family, every member of which was affected in one way or another. Survivors hope you will never let anyone make light of that. They want you to realize that many of them lived surrounded by death, and witnessed the death toll rise with their own eyes. The number of victims is not exaggerated.

Chapter Four

The Dehumanization of the European Jew

All European Jews were victims during Hitler's reign, whether they were deported to concentration camps or not. They were all oppressed long before the deportations began, as they were stripped of their citizenship and their rights a little more each day, and subjected to humiliation, harsh rules and often brutal treatment. Survivors want you to understand that even if they were not in camps or in hiding, they also were not necessarily free.

On September 15, 1935, new laws were announced, which according to Sir Martin Gilbert, Holocaust historian and writer, "elevated random discrimination into a system." (p.47) Beginning with laws that defined "Reich Citizenship," Jews were no longer considered German citizens, but rather subjects of the state, and not of "German blood," so they could no longer fly the German flag, regardless of how far back their family lineage might go in Germany.

The Nuremberg Race Laws established the definition of a Jew. "Jews with three or four Jewish grandparents were considered full-blooded Jews." (Yad Vashem) If a person had two Jewish grandparents, but was not married to a Jew or did not attend a synagogue, he or she was known as a Mischlinge (part-Jew), and this category was later broken into varying degrees, for example, separately distinguishing those having only one Jewish grandparent. This was an interesting means of categorization when you realize that Judaism is a religion and not a race, so in reality, there was no Jewish "blood line" on which to base this classification system. (Aretha, 2009. p.86)

Hitler, however, chose to define Judaism as race, rather than a religion. If it were simply a religion, Jews could convert, thus taking away his excuse to eliminate them. Once he made it about the bloodline, genetics, there was no getting away from that, so they were doomed whether they had ever set foot in a synagogue or not.

As a result of Hitler's bloodline beliefs, Germans could not marry nor have intimate relations outside of marriage with Jews. They were to be excluded from German life, even though they themselves were German. Soon, Germans began taking over Jewish businesses, or worded more pleasantly, "They were being transferred into Aryan hands." (Martin p.50)

Jews were soon prohibited from holding public office, teaching school, and voting. They could not fight any longer in the German Armed Forces. Jewish doctors could no longer practice medicine at German government hospitals. Additionally, Jews were banned from public places such as movie theaters, parks, and restaurants. Jewish lawyers could no longer practice.

Photo Credit: Public Domain

Restrictions were placed on the times Jews could leave their homes. For example, they had to remain inside between the hours of 6:00 PM and 8:00 AM. Shopping was also limited as they were only permitted to patronize businesses owned by non-Jews between the hours of 3:00 PM and 5:00 PM. When they were out, they could not use public telephones or own their own, ride public transportation, or own private transportation. They had to surrender their radios and bicycles to the Nazis, were no longer permitted to walk on the sidewalks, and instead were relegated to the gutters.

Jews had to turn over their gold and silver to the government and were only allowed to keep a small amount of their own money. They had to wear identifiable Stars of David upon every article of clothing.

Photo Credit: Public Domain

These are just some of the laws, listed in no particular order, imposed upon the European Jewish population as early as 1935. Clearly, life was difficult for them long before the mass deportations occurred.

Holocaust survivors were not free prior to their deportations. All of their rights were stripped from them one by one until they were treated like the vermin the Nazis accused them of being. Without these rights, they continued to exist, struggled to survive, and endured, thinking it surely couldn't get any worse, but before too long, the situation did indeed get worse with the introduction of the ghettos in several areas.

As early as 1939, the Nazis developed areas in key cities where they could concentrate all of the Jews of that vicinity. The conditions were horrible. Several families were often forced into a single apartment. Food was scarce, and they were surrounded by filth and human waste. Usually, they were not permitted to leave, and before long, no one was allowed in to take any provisions to them. Ghettos were walled off and heavily guarded. Many Jews died within the walls of a ghetto.

Little could they know that this was a just a precursor to the camps that many would find themselves in later. As the ghettos over-filled due to an influx of people forced in from other areas, deportations began to "make room."

It is important that you know that European Jews did not have the same freedoms as those in other parts of the world. They did not usually go from happy home to concentration camp. They suffered, went hungry, and had little control of their own lives for years first, and nothing was done to help them. Neighbors watched instead of fighting their forced removal, often with little to no warning, and then often took over their homes and belongings following their departure.

Jewish Section- Photo Credit: Public Domain

Chapter Five

Like Lambs to the Slaughter

Despite popular belief, not all Jews went with their captors willingly "like lambs to the slaughter." Perhaps there were people of the Jewish population who peacefully followed the commands of the Nazis as they forced them into captivity. They are, after all, a peace loving people, but one must not take this as a sign of weakness. In some cases, they could be accused of being a bit too naive or too trusting of the bogus promises that were made to them. We must remember that the Nazi regime was very good at telling lies, using propaganda, and staging, so perhaps some Jews wanted to believe them and take them at their word when they were told that they were being "relocated" and that "their needs would be provided for," but we must never take that as weakness.

In the book, *Inside the Gas Chambers*, Shlomo Venezia, a former member of a Sonderkommando in Auschwitz, explains that it was not difficult for the Nazis to deport the Jews living in Greece who were already living with food shortages and were used to seeing young and healthy citizens taken away to do labor, and saw them later returned. Therefore the round ups were not new to them.

They were not very political, and thought that the Germans "were precise, decent people." He claims that, "They didn't have enough to eat, and here people were offering them a place to live in exchange for their labor-it didn't seem like such a big deal." (Venezia, 2009. P.10)

Those who did go peacefully, wanted only to cooperate to save their families. They protected their families the best they could with limited resources until the very end. It is not as if these people kept semi-automatic weapons in their homes with which to fight back aggressively. Even if they had, they would have been far outnumbered and their weaponry would not compare to that of the German Army. Considering these circumstances, they were not at all weak, but in fact, they were quite strong. They had strong convictions and strong faith, conviction that good would triumph over evil, and strong faith that God would see them through and put an end to the madness.

Warsaw Ghetto Uprising. The original German caption reads:"Forcibly pulled out of dug-outs." Public domain. Photo credit: Jürgen Stroop Report to Heinrich Himmler from May 1943

However, not all tried to cooperate. Some fought with everything they had in them, and this resistance took on many forms. From forged documents, underground newspapers, and going into hiding to sabotage by partisans and uprisings in ghettos and concentration camps, Jews absolutely did courageously fight back. Of course, any who had the means to leave Nazi occupied areas or areas in Hitler's path, while it was still permitted, did flee. For most though, it was not an option.

Of those who had to stay, altering documents was one means of trying to survive a little longer. According to the University of Minnesota Center for Holocaust and Genocide Studies, "Forged or faked documents were yet another way to stay alive, especially for Jews assuming false identities. Baptismal, birth and marriage certificates masked the religion of Jews and offered them a chance to pass as Christians." The university's webpage goes on to say that according to historian Martin Gilbert, 800,000 Jews did manage to escape or find refuge. Many of those were in large part due to forged documents. (Fromowitz, 2005)

Some Jews found places to hide. For adults, this wasn't as easy as it was for the children. The parents of these children often had to make the difficult decision to find someone to take their children, knowing full-well that there was a great chance that they would not survive to be with them again, but people were willing to take them in and hide them. Christian families often took in these children and taught them Christian prayers and practices. They would change the children's names, and raise them as their own, which often put the protectors at great personal risk. For the children, regardless of whether they were taken in by another family or places such as boarding schools, convents, or orphanages, it meant being suddenly thrown together with people they most likely did not know, while being stripped from their parents and the security of their homes. For parents, in addition to realizing their chance for a reunion was not great, they also knew that they ran the risk of their small children forgetting them by the time everything was calm again one day.

Some adults found hiding places as well, and we will look more closely at some of the heroes who made this possible in the next chapter. For now, suffice it to say that not everyone who risked his or her life to hide Jews was famous. Those who did choose to help had varying motives from moral obligations to financial gain. For example, non-Jewish Polish famers would hide Jewish children from nearby villages, for a price, and only until it became too dangerous for their own good.

Rather than go into hiding, other Jews began to fight back. One form of resistance that increased as time went on was the underground communication network established by some of the Jewish ghetto residents. Underground groups formed, and they began printing newspapers, writing diaries, having concerts and plays, and running schools, among other illegal activities, right under the noses of the Nazis.

As violence started to build and deportations increase, some of the same Jews turned to armed resistance. In Jewish ghettos, inhabitants armed themselves and resisted the Nazis upon learning that plans were underway to empty the ghettos by deporting all remaining residents to concentration camps. In time, resistance turned to revolt in places like Warsaw.

Established in November of 1940, the Warsaw Ghetto was a small section of the city of Warsaw, Poland to which all Warsaw Jews, at one point numbering nearly 400,000, were forced to relocate. A wall was built, and the entrances heavily guarded by Nazi soldiers. Jews were not allowed outside of the 10-foot wall, and before long, this rule was reinforced under threat of the death penalty. (The American Experience, PBS, 1994)

Living conditions within the ghetto were awful. According to the United States Holocaust Memorial Museum, "German authorities forced ghetto residents to live in an area of 1.3 square miles, with an average of 7.2 persons per room." (USHMM Warsaw, 2013) Unable to buy food, the inhabitants had to rely on the Nazis to provide for them. The Nazis barely provided enough to keep them alive. Medical and fuel supplies also ran short, and before long disease spread throughout. According to *American Experience: America and the Holocaust* matters got worse when the sewer pipes froze, and people began throwing excrement in the streets. (PBS.1994)

By 1942, thousands of Jews were dying of disease each month, and 6000 per day were being transported to Treblinka. The Jews were told they were going to work camps, but soon word spread that the truth was they were headed to the extermination camp of Treblinka. The Jewish Combat Organization (ZOB), an underground movement, along with other groups, purchased weapons and prepared to ambush the Nazis. (History Channel, n.d.) When the Germans arrived with the intention of transporting thousands to the extermination camps, the resistance fighters ambushed.

Within days of the start of the uprising, German forces were able to break through the resistance, but some resistors continued to hide and fight off the Germans for close to a month, but sadly, in the end, they did not prevail. Although they managed to kill approximately 300 German soldiers, their ammunition supply dwindled, without which, they were no match against the German Army. In the end, approximately 7000 of the remaining Jews of Warsaw, both the resistance fighters and those citizens who were in hiding, were killed as the Germans destroyed the bunkers in which they were hidden. Another estimated 7000 were sent to Treblinka to be killed. Those who remained were sent to labor and concentration camps. (USHMM.org)

Jews captured during the Warsaw ghetto uprising. Warsaw, Poland, Apr.19-May 16, 1943.*National Archives and Records Administration, College Park, Md.*

Additionally, according to the United States Holocaust Memorial Museum, some 20,000-30,000 Jews, many resistance fighters already, were able to escape to forests where they formed partisan units. Not only did they hide effectively while living outside in the woods, but they were still able to amass arms and fight with the Allies or sabotage the Nazis on their own by blowing up train tracks. Near Vilna, they were able to kill over 3000 German soldiers and derail hundreds of trains. (USHMM Jewish partisans)

Inspired by the resistance of Warsaw, still others fought the guards in the extermination camps. From blowing up one of the crematoriums in Birkenau, to revolting and sometimes escaping Sobibor and Treblinka killing camps, inmates stood up to their captors. Unfortunately, most were recaptured and killed, but those who survived have served as an invaluable resource for helping us understand exactly how horrific these camps truly were. Generally, these escapees were members of the Sonderkommando, those prisoners selected to do the Nazi's dirty work, as described earlier. The fact that they did this work is the only reason that they were alive at all. Taking a final stand, they courageously stood up to the guards, causing destruction and fleeing from a hopeless situation.

Former entrance to Sobibor extermination camp (photo: public domain)

There were certainly other forms of resistance such as spiritual resistance in the ghettos and camps. Jews secretly continued their prayers, studies, and holiday celebrations in whatever way they could manage. All of this was clearly not permitted by the Nazis, so even such mild forms of resistance could result in death; yet, everything from art to diary entries to plays were smuggled out of the camps to provide us with first-hand accounts of life in there, and of the resistance shown by courageously risking their lives to get those accounts to the outside world.

Holocaust survivors would like you to know that they did not all go quietly like lambs to the slaughter. They were not in any way weak. In fact, they were probably stronger than many of us. In whatever manner each could, all fought in their own ways, both emotionally and physically, until the very end.

Three participants in the Treblinka uprising who escaped and survived the war. Warsaw, Poland, 1945. *US Holocaust Memorial Museum*

Chapter Six

The Tragedy of Indifference

Hitler had a great deal of help in his quest for domination, and some of that assistance came from surprising and unlikely sources such as support from well-known companies, including American companies, and from the leaders of other countries. Not all support took on the same form, though. Some of the support that aided Hitler was that of indifference from individual citizens and from world leaders.

Prisoners at forced labor in the Siemens factory. Auschwitz camp, Poland,1940-1944. *Federation Nationale des Deportes et Internes Resistants et Patriots* © United States Holocaust Memorial Museum, Washington, DC

One of the greatest tragedies of our world is when people witness injustice at any level and don't do anything about it, and that was one of the biggest crimes of the Holocaust. When people turn their heads or say nothing as wrongs are committed, it is as if they are supporting the acts of the perpetrator. Edmund Burke once said, "All that is necessary for the triumph of evil is that good men do nothing." This happened all too often during Hitler's regime.

Often, fear kept average citizens from doing more to help the victims or stand up to the Nazis. Certainly, their fears were well-founded. The punishment for any display of betrayal toward Hitler was indeed harsh and often resulted in incarceration in a concentration camp or possibly even death. The threat of which, however, did not deter everyone. There are several documented acts of resistance against the Nazis and accounts of people willing to risk everything to help the Jews. Some of these will be discussed in the next chapter. These acts of resistance, however, were not enough to stop the powerful dictator, so what might have stopped him?

Perhaps had other countries been more flexible on their immigration policies, more Jews could have escaped and found refuge. This was not the case, and early on when some might have actually still had the opportunity to escape, many had their visas denied or were turned away. One example of a group of refugees turned away from more than one safe haven is the *S.S. St. Louis*, which in May of 1939, the spring following Kristallnacht, was scheduled to take German Jewish refugees to Cuba. Some of these refugees even came out of hiding at great risk in order to board the ship. The ship sailed on May 13th, 1939, but by May 23rd the captain received a message that the passengers might not be able to land in Cuba as planned because of a new decree, Decree 937, that essentially nullified the landing permits that had cost passengers vast amounts of money to secure their right to land there. They were unable to land as issues were hashed out between leaders, and fear set in amongst the passengers that they may be sent back to Germany and ultimately, to the concentration camps.

During this tense and unstable time, some people attempted suicide rather than face what awaited them should they have to return to Nazi controlled Germany. Eventually word came that they were denied entry to Cuba, and all negations were closed. Finally, the Joint Distribution Committee (JDC) was able to work with other countries that agreed to allow in some of the refugees. Great Britain agreed to take 228, Belgium would take 214, Holland accepted 181, and 224 could go to France. (Jewish Virtual Library U.S. Policy During the Holocaust: The Tragedy of S.S. St. Louis)

Noticeably missing on that list of countries is America. The United States, as tensions heightened in Germany, was in the midst of a deep economic depression. Its citizens and leaders were apprehensive about taking in immigrants, which would strain an already struggling economy and create even more competition for limited resources and job opportunities. Such apprehension led to inflexibility in immigration policies. Worse though, was that the man in charge of the Visa Division of the U.S. State Department was anti-Semitic and managed to reverse the orders of President Roosevelt, which would have eased the restrictions on immigration allowing more European Jews to find refuge in America. Rather, Breckinridge Long's maneuvers resulted in tightening immigration restrictions. According to *America and the Holocaust*,

> Long designed a secret policy to tighten the immigration requirements, effectively slashing admissions by half. A year later, Long's department cut refugee immigration once more, this time reducing admission to about a quarter of the relevant quotas. (American Experience, PBS. 1994)

At one point the St. Louis sailed along the coast of Florida. The passengers aboard could even see the lights of Miami. Some of them sent messages to President Franklin D. Roosevelt, asking that they be accepted into the United States, but he never responded. (USHMM)

America was not alone in its reluctance to take in these refugees, though. It seemed as if only the Dominican Republic, and to some extent Boliva, were willing to admit significant numbers of refugees. Had other countries been more willing, what difference might have been made?

Perhaps all of the efforts in the world may not have actually been able to stop Hitler, we can never know for sure, but more lives could have been saved had anti-Semitic attitudes changed, immigration quotas lifted or eased, and differences been tolerated. These steps would have shown that his methods were not approved of, nor accepted.

Anti-Semitism was not an invention of Hitler's. It existed long before he came to power, but at his prompting, and through an aggressive propaganda campaign led by his Propaganda Minister Joseph Goebbels, evidence of it quickly exacerbated. Before long, not only were non-Jewish neighbors not protecting the Jews they may have known their entire lives, but many began to turn on them, even going as far as to report their whereabouts to the Germans. As mentioned earlier, there were many people who did step in and do something by hiding Jews or assisting in finding them passage to safety, but if more had taken this risk, how many more might have been saved? If neighbor had not turned against neighbor, how many generations of families might have been spared?

Sadly, for the passengers of the *St. Louis*, finding refuge in other countries of Europe was only a temporary reprieve. At least half of those were returned to that continent, and even though not sent back to Germany, still perished in the Holocaust as country after country was invaded by the Germans.

Unfortunately, indifference continues to plague our world today. People often think only of themselves or their immediate circle of friends, family, and associates, and feel that it is not their place to intervene with things that do not involve them. As a result, perpetrators from bullies in the school hallways to tyrannical leaders of certain countries continue to get away with cruel behaviors because they are not stopped.

As students stand by and watch the school bully without speaking up or countries stand by and do not address a tyrannical leader because it is "not our problem," the perpetrator may see it as a sign of support. In his or her eyes, the behavior is obviously accepted, even agreed with, or someone would put a stop to it. When we quietly watch injustices without speaking up for fear of causing any ripples, we potentially contribute to a future tidal wave.

Elie Wiesel once said in a speech, "I swore never to be silent whenever and wherever human beings endure suffering and humiliation. We must take sides. Neutrality helps the oppressor, never the victim. Silence encourages the tormentor, never the tormented. For the dead and the living, we must bear witness." (Elie Wiesel from his speech when given the Nobel Peace Prize)

Holocaust survivors wonder why the world was silent and wish more people would have spoken up against the atrocities they suffered at the hands of the Nazis. They want you to know the importance of speaking out in the face of injustice.

Refugees aboard the "St. Louis" wait to hear whether Cuba will grant them entry. Off the coast of Havana, Cuba, June 3, 1939.—*National Archives and Records Administration, College Park, Md.*

Chapter Seven

The Rescuers

Fortunately, there are people who stood up against Adolf Hitler and the rest of the Nazis and who rescued Jews. While, their actions did not stop Hitler, they did save lives and as a result, future generations. Here we will look at just a few of them.

Miep Gies is probably one of the most well-known "rescuers" of World War II. Together with other co-workers, she took care of Anne Frank and her family along with the Van Pels family and Fritz Pfeffer while they were in hiding in Amsterdam. Although a loyal employee of Mr. Otto Frank, Gies went above and beyond the call of duty to secure

Ration cards, buy food and supplies, and keep up the morale of those in hiding for more than two years.

It is also Miep who saved the now-famous diary of Anne Frank and was able to return it to Anne's father Otto upon his return from Auschwitz concentration camp. At great risk to her own life, this non-Jewish young newlywed never hesitated when Mr. Frank asked for her assistance and candor. After learning that the remainder of his family had not survived, Otto Frank even stayed with Gies and her husband for seven years after his liberation from Auschwitz. Frank and Miep remained friends until the time of Otto's death in 1980.

Miep died at the age of 100, and in all of the years in between the war and her death, she actively wrote and spoke of her experiences and shared Anne Frank's messages with thousands of people.

Corrie ten Boom is also famous for her fearless acts of courage in hiding many Jews in her home in the Netherlands. The full story is told in the book and movie of the same name, *The Hiding Place*. Corrie, along with her sister Betsie and father Casper ran a clock repair business in the front of their home in Haarlem, Netherlands. They were a well-known and respected Christian family, who began to take in Jewish people and hide them in their home. Although not of the Jewish faith, they respectfully honored Jewish traditions for the refugees they harbored, such as observing the Sabbath and serving kosher food. To be shown such respect in a time when most Jews were treated like they were of no value was both rare and appreciated.

The ten Booms even went as far as to have their house retrofitted to accommodate a large hiding space within the wall where the Jews could escape if anyone showed up looking for them at the business or house unexpectedly. In fact, that little room was packed with six refugees when the ten Boom family was arrested, all six went undetected, and were rescued and taken to new hiding places two days later, and all but one survived the war. (Corrie ten Boom)

Corrie, Betsie, and Casper were eventually found out and turned in by Dutch informants, a disturbing and unfortunately all-too-common act, and arrested. They were taken to various concentration camps where Casper died early on, followed by Betsie who died while she and Corrie were in Ravensbruck camp in Germany, but Corrie survived and was released in December of 1944.

Upon her return, Corrie set up homes to house jobless Dutch and Holocaust survivors. She was knighted by Holland's queen, and she then shared her story through writing books and speaking around the world until stripped of that ability by debilitating strokes. She lived to be 91 years old. Today, the ten Boom home and business stand as a museum where visitors can view the secret room.

Sir Nicholas Winton is a humble and unassuming hero of the Holocaust. His story is one of my favorites for just that reason. Until the 1980s when his wife stumbled across a scrap book in their attic, his story was unknown even to her. The book was from 1939 and contained the pictures, names, and information of children he had helped escape Nazi-controlled regions of Europe. He had never told anyone about his efforts, keeping his secret for decades.

Finally, the story of how Winton coordinated Kinder Transports to rescue almost 700 children from Czechoslovakia and get them to safety in Great Brittan just before World War II began was made public. This led to a tear-jerking appearance on the show *That's Life* during which, he was surprised by an audience full of people who were alive only as a result of Winton's courageous actions. Among his many honors since his story went public, he has been named as one of the Righteous Among the Nations at Yad Vashem in Israel and was knighted by Queen Elizabeth II. At the time of this writing, he had just celebrated his 105th birthday!

Children who arrived in Great Britain on Children's Transports (Kinder transporte) from Germany and Austriatake a meal in Harwich. Great Britain, December 14,1938—*Wide World Photo* Copyright © United States Holocaust Memorial Museum, Washington, DC

Irena Sendler was a nurse and social worker in Warsaw, Poland. She is credited with developing a plan to get into the Warsaw Ghetto during the Nazi occupation under the guise of inspecting the sanitary conditions for the municipality. Once inside, she developed relations with the Jewish underground and began the process of smuggling Jews, particularly children, out and finding hiding places for them.

She kept records of those children who had to be taken away from their parents and brought to safety. She found clever ways to hide these documents, such as burying them in jars in the ground. As a result of these efforts, she was imprisoned, and was once even beaten so severely that she was left for dead. Sendler's harrowing story has been told in many books and movies including the 2011 documentary *Irena Sendler: In the Name of Their Mothers* for PBS.

Although we can see that one person really can make a difference in the lives of many, sometimes it actually does "take a village." The village of **Le Chambon-sur-Lignon**, and surrounding villages, in France were instrumental in harboring refugees, approximately 5,000, from 1940-1944. The story of the impact this village had in saving so many people is told in detail on http://www.auschwitz.dk/Trocme.htm, but here, I will share just a portion with you to demonstrate the courage of the village residents. (The Village)

Ordinary people, often poverty-stricken themselves, protected the Jews at the peril of risking their own lives. They took the Jews into their homes and fed and protected them, right under the noses of the Gestapo. Defying the Nazi régime and their collaborators, the French government, the villagers of the area of Le Chambon provided a welcoming refuge throughout the war for the Jews. Every home hid strangers, not for days, but for years. So deep was their humanity that no resident of Le Chambon ever turned away, denounced, or betrayed a single Jewish refugee.

Jewish children sheltered by the Protestant population of the village of Le Chambon-sur-Lignon. France, 1941. *US Holocaust Memorial Museum*

A group of children who were sheltered in Le Chambon-sur-Lignon, a town in southern France. Le Chambon-sur-Lignon, France, August 1942. — *US Holocaust Memorial Museum*

I would love to think that if similar situations should ever arise, people would rally in this way and risk their lives to save others, but I'm sure my thinking is overly optimistic. Too many people today turn their heads and look away from injustice because it is an inconvenience to do otherwise.

If you take the time to look at the numbers of Jews pre and post-war, the near destruction of European Jewry is evident. Some places show far greater losses than others. For example, Poland lost 3,000,000 of its 3,300,000 Jews. The Netherlands lost 100,000 of its 140,000. Yet Denmark lost just 60 of its 8000. Certainly those 60 lives should never have been taken, but the ratio of those who lived to those who died is indeed low when compared to other countries. What was the difference?

The main difference is that the Danish people protected their Jews, unlike some of the other countries where the Gentile population would turn against them and even betray them to the Nazis. Danish resistance workers helped hide them and then get them to the shore, where they would be put on boats and smuggled out to Sweden, which was a neutral country. All of this hiding and transport was done right under the noses of the Nazis. According to the United States Holocaust Memorial Museum, "Over a period of about a month, some 7,200 Jews and 700 of their non-Jewish relatives, traveled to safety in Sweden, which accepted the Danish refugees." When the Nazis looked, they were hard-pressed to find Jews in hiding in Denmark. (Rescue, 2013)

Holocaust survivors want you to be aware that many of them owe their lives and those of their children and grandchildren to brave individuals and groups who made moral choices to do what is right for humanity, not what is popular, or what is safe, but they courageously did what they knew had to be done without hesitation and at great personal risk.

Members of a Polish family who hid a Jewish girl on their farm. Zyrardow, Poland, 1941-1942.
— *US Holocaust Memorial Museum*

Danish fishermen (foreground) ferry a boat load of fugitive across a narrow sound to Sweden.

Jewish children who had been hidden in convents, Poland-Yad Vashem Photo Archive, 1644/106

Chapter Eight

Judgment and Anti-Semitism

Has the Holocaust taught us nothing at all? Sometimes it does appear that way. For if it had, how could people possibly still judge others on the basis of their differences? During their speeches, Holocaust survivors often convey strong feelings about the need to treat everyone with respect despite differences in race, religion, color, or anything else. Many times, I have watched a Holocaust survivor look directly into the eyes of students and in still prevalent European Yiddish accents say, "Never judge! We are all the same. It doesn't matter what color our skin is or what religion we are. We are all the same, and don't judge anyone who is different."

Ideals such as racism, anti-Semitism, extreme hatred, bigotry, and stereotyping are part of the judgments that can lead a person or group to thinking that it has superiority over another, and they often stem from fear, insecurity, or hatred. When someone belittles others because of differences, he or she fills the role of superior and treats others as subordinates. If outspoken enough, the person in the role of superior can espouse his or her hatred and ideas on friends, relatives, acquaintances, and if convincing, persuade others to agree and perhaps act upon their hatred. This pattern is still evident today in groups such as the Ku Klux Klan, Neo-Nazi-style white supremacist groups, and even with religious zealots. Wherever the idea exists that we are all not created equal, no good can prevail. This is one lesson from the Holocaust that survivors wish people would realize. They don't want anyone to judge another for any reason or difference because they know all too well where it can lead.

No one has the right to judge another person, but we are all guilty of doing it at some level. Perhaps we make comments on someone's clothing or hair style. Maybe we criticize someone's actions. It is hard to say why this comes so naturally to some. Do they really think that they are that much better than someone else, or is it perhaps that finding fault in others makes their own inadequacies seem more trivial? These may seem like minor offences, but this is where separations begin. This is where the feelings of superiority sprout, and left unchecked, they can lead to more serious negative thought patterns such as prejudice and hatred.

Judgment is alarmingly prevalent in today's schools. Students are bullied and hazed based on race, religion, sexual orientation, and appearance. While it is true that bullying has always existed, and most of us lived through one form of it or another as children, the reach of the bully goes further today and results in more traumatic consequences.

With the implementation of the Internet, cell phones, and social media, the bully has a more vast audience. No longer are the incidents just witnessed by a handful of students in the play yard or hallway. Text messages, Tweets, and Facebook posts can reach hundreds of potential followers, and with each click of a "Like" button, the bully gains strength.

The devastating results of such far-reaching torment can have dire consequences. In the article "Stop Bullying Not Judging People Because of Their Race Religion Sexual Identity Or By Looks and Body Type Size," Rye Catcher states:

> Many young people are killing themselves because of bullying, hazing, teasing and other practices that are forms of harassment. Teens and kids do not feel safe in their schools or on their neighborhood streets. They fear ridicule, humiliation and fear in the places that they should feel the most safe. (Catcher)

Tolerance is not enough to solve the issue of dangerous judgments. It is not enough to say, "Okay, you are different than I am, but I can accept you." That still denotes an air of superiority and implies that one person is better than another. One should never have to feel "tolerated." We need to not only avoid fearing the differences, not only accept them, but appreciate and learn from them. All types of people deserve to be respected for who and what they are.

In some cases, the fact that this lesson has not been heeded frustrates survivors, because if the Holocaust didn't teach them about where ideas of inequality, superiority, or extreme hatred can lead, what will it take? Nobel Peace Prize winner and Holocaust surviving Professor Elie Wiesel said in an interview with Professor Georg Klein that the world has not learned anything from Auschwitz (the largest of the concentration/ extermination camps). Wiesel never imagined that years after the liberation of the concentration camp in 1945, the world would still be battling racism, anti-Semitism, and the starvation of children. Yet, here we are with the same problems all of these many years later. (Klein, 2004) Many other survivors are in disbelief of this lack of lessons learned. Most likely that is why they continue to speak out. They hope that someday their words will hit the right ears, and someone will eventually listen.

None of us have the right to determine what is considered acceptable behavior for others, the perfect look for them, or the right religion for them to follow. We must learn to accept others' differences in a respectful and kind way, and embrace those differences. Yet, these types of judgments appear every day, and they lead to anti-Semitic acts.

Accept diversity. Photo: Public Domain

Unbelievably, in many places where heroic survivors of the Shoah tirelessly speak in an effort to educate people about the atrocities of the Holocaust, they are confronted by protestors. All of these years later, they must still suffer at the hands of those who for whatever reason feel superior to Jewish people. Survivors want you to open your eyes and see that anti-Semitism still exists and still poses a threat to Jews worldwide. In addition to harassing 80 to 90 year-old survivors, these intolerant individuals and groups also target synagogues, Jewish schools, and Jewish community centers committing crimes from defacing property and fire bombs to drive-by shootings. Watching the nightly news provides glimpses of such anti-Semitic acts from around the world from burning mezuzahs in Brooklyn, New York to synagogue arsons in New Jersey. As such acts decrease in some places in the world, they increase in others. Understanding how anyone can have such severe hatred for another based entirely on race or religion is unfathomable, but trying to make sense of killings spurned from such loathing is nearly impossible.

As a civilized society, we should be far more evolved by now. Following years of slavery and the ugly battles for its abolishment, the fight for civil rights, and the vast numbers who perished during the Holocaust, we should all be committed to never letting racist and anti-Semitic attitudes prevail ever again. The fact that any such incidents still happen is disturbing.

In the month that I finished this book in 2014, there was an incident in Japan, which involved the destruction of more than one hundred copies of Anne Frank's *The Diary of a Young Girl,* as well as some other books of related information. According to Arden Dier of *Newser*, in "Japan Mystery: Anne Frank's Diary Torn Apart," in 31 of Tokyo's libraries, 265 books on Anne Frank and the Holocaust were vandalized. (Dier, 2014) This is one of many clear acts of recent anti-Semitism.

Anti-Semitic graffiti on a college dormitory door.
Photo: Public Domain

Additionally, Fox News.com recently reported the story of a Jewish teacher in Paris who was brutally attacked, and a Swastika drawn on his chest. The article "Victim of savage anti-Semitic attack in Paris recounts beating" shows the severity of this anti-Semitic event. (Victim of savage, 2014)

Almost daily, we can turn on the news and see stories such as these. Anti-Semitic events take place all of the world and close to home. Recently, three people were killed by a lone gunman, later found to have White Supremacist and Ku Klux Klan ties. He shot a man and his grandson at a Jewish Community Center, and one woman at a Jewish retirement home. Ironically, his randomly selected victims were Christian. It is a shame that in our so-called civilized world that even I have to keep crimes such as his in mind as I volunteer at a Holocaust museum that shares a campus with a Jewish Community Center. I have to be cautious every time I open the door to admit a patron. The threat of anti-Semitic violence is real though, and one that I must remain cognizant of whenever I work there. Fortunately, there is security present.

Also during the writing of this book, a group of people in the Ukraine began to pass out fliers at Jewish synagogues declaring that all Jews over age 16 had to register their religion and pay a fee or face having their property taken and deportation. The fliers were intended to as if they came from the new Ukrainian government, but were found to be fraudulent. Nevertheless, the act was quite disturbing.

In New York City, a cab driver has been seen wearing an arm band that boasts a Swastika on his left arm. It is visible through the driver's side window, sending a clear message to potential passengers that certain clientele are not wanted.

He has been suspended for wearing the arm band and insists he will continue to wear it anyway, just not while driving the cab. Claiming that he is not anti-Semitic and feeling that his rights are being violated, he voiced the following: "I don't hate Jews. I'm critical of them, but I don't hate them," he claimed. "That doesn't mean that I'm anti-Semitic. That don't make me a hater." He also pointed out, "I know it's very controversial that a non-white is wearing a Nazi armband," he said. "Whoever said you had to be white to be a National Socialist?" (Dvorin, 2014)

A recent study showed 554 violent anti-Semitic acts in 2013, which included attacks on people, synagogues, and Jewish cemeteries and other institutions, and in some areas, they have increased dramatically so far in 2014. The report of researchers at Tel Aviv University "warns that racist and anti-Semitic attitudes are becoming more acceptable, particularly among European youths." They provide the example of an inverted Nazi salute that has been made at Nazi concentration camps and in front of Anne Frank's homes. (David, 2014)

How is this possible? How can people be so heartless, so anti-Semitic, and so full of hatred after all that happened during the Holocaust? It terrifies me when I think of how little was learned in the face of such atrocities. What is even more frightening is that in the most recent European elections, neo-Nazi parties won two seats, just one day after three people getting shot to death in front of a synagogue. Neo-Nazis holding a government office is incredibly troubling to me.

Photo credit: Israel News Agency

History is repeating itself before our eyes, and I can't help but wonder where, or even if, it will stop? Whether or not anti-Semitic actions are sanctioned by a government or radical individuals, the fact that there are groups of people out there who think this way is just sickening.

In *Dachau 29 April 1945*, liberator PFC Sam S. Platamone is quoted from a 1996 letter as saying, “Man’s inhumanity to man continues.” That realization must be most distressing for a witness of the atrocities of the Nazis against the inmates of Dachau. Unfortunately, his observation still holds true today. (Dann, 1998. P. 123)

Holocaust survivors want you to speak up and raise awareness against these actions. If we don't, it looks to the perpetrators as if this behavior is accepted, and when looking to the past, you can see where that can lead. Whether you are Jewish or not, speak out and support those people who are threatened by radical groups and individuals, especially Holocaust survivors. They have been through enough, and should not have to suffer from having old wounds reopened. No one should.

Chapter Nine

The Gift of Education

As a teacher, it can be frustrating to watch students who care so little about the education that they receive for free. I must admit that I was that type of student once upon a time myself. Like so many things today, especially here in America, we take our educational opportunities for granted. Considering how many people have had the chance for an education ripped away from them, such apathy is shameful. Holocaust survivors often wish they could have completed their own schooling when they should have been able to do so.

The interruption of education was a gradual process. At first, Jews were discriminated against and bullied. They were harassed and humiliated. Sadly, it was not only at the hands of non-Jewish students. Much of the harassment was instigated by the teachers. Jews in a certain area may have been forced to switch schools, perhaps taking them away from the only school they had ever known. Then, they were prohibited from attending school at all. When some Jewish families tried to continue their education by hiring private teachers or tutors, they paid a heavy price, often at the cost of the life of the teacher, and perhaps the entire family that hired that teacher, from infants to grandparents. Nazis would publicly kill the family to discourage other families from attempting the same practice.

German Jewish children were often made to stand at the front of the class as the teacher pointed out that they were 'different' © 2011 Yad Vashem The Holocaust Martyrs' and Heroes' Remembrance Authority

Adding further insult to injury, Jews were banned from entering a public library, and curfews were imposed, which left precious little time available for them to leave their homes at all. Therefore, the opportunity for any form of alternative education such as self-study or study groups with friends or former classmates was also not plausible.

Finally, in most cases, all hope of an education was thwarted when Jews were taken from their homes and sent to ghettos or to labor, concentration, or extermination camps. For those who survived, it can be frustrating to see how little some students care about school. Today's students are entitled to an education, at least here in America, and they are well-aware of that. Many students give it little thought or perhaps, even resent it. They know school will always be there for them and may even dread having to go there each day. Holocaust survivors who had their educational options taken away all together, in most cases, would have given anything to continue going to school.

A first-grade class at a Jewish school. Cologne, Germany, 1929-1930. *US Holocaust Memorial Museum*

One survivor I know lost so much in the Holocaust, a home, family members, freedom, and yet she never seems angry when she discusses any of these losses. When she discusses her education though, she gets an incredibly bitter tone in her voice. Others I have met take on similar tones when discussing the subject. Their anger builds the more they discuss the opportunities that they lost due a lack of education.

When I see this transformation in the demeanor of survivors, I am amazed. It is as if the entire ordeal happened only yesterday. In the case of my friend, she is one of the sweetest people I know, and to look at her, you would never guess the hardships that she has lived through, but mention school or education, particularly how lightly students today take it, and she gets fired up immediately.

On one occasion, I have personally witnessed a Holocaust survivor act a bit jealous or even bitter toward another. The survivor who was a guest speaker at an event that I attended, spoke of how she had the opportunity to go on to receive her education because she survived after leaving her home country on a Kinder Transport. She had become a teacher and later a school principal. Following her speech, several of us went up to meet her personally, and I watched as another survivor described her own situation and how she was not as fortunate and did not get the chance for an education. She explained that she was unable to escape, and instead suffered through the camps. Watching them compare hardships and losses, I realized just how much resentment some survivors have for having schooling denied them, and how envious they can be of those who received their full education.

In addition to the young children who were deprived of schooling, I think of young adult European Jews who were taken to the camps as they were in their final year of college. Such promising lives cut short. What might they have become had they been able to complete their college studies? We could have more Nobel Prize winners, award-winning artists, writers, or musicians. To have made it to the college level, these young people must have been passionate about something, and obviously they cared a great deal about their education.

The importance of education has been paramount in my own adult life, but admittedly, I had never given much thought to how I would feel if the opportunity had been taken away from me until I began talking to survivors. Only then did I realize how much opportunity I have and how much I have selfishly taken for granted. Children of today need to learn this lesson, and fortunately some of our Holocaust survivors are still with us and willing to share for as long as they still are able to do so.

Holocaust survivors hope you never take your education for granted. You should appreciate all of the educational opportunities available to you, and take advantage of each one.

Chapter Ten

Good Germans?

Despite the harsh treatment at the hands of most Nazis and the anti-Semitism with which they must still contend, most of the Holocaust survivors I have spoken with want you to know that not all Germans were bad. As a matter of fact, many will discuss times that Germans saved their lives at great risk to their own.

My conversations with survivors have included stories of various Nazis who helped them, and yes, even saved their lives. This took many forms such as the smuggling of food, providing medicine for an illness, or occasionally helping them move to a better barrack or working assignment. The survivors who have shared these stories with me, want it known there were some "good Germans."

One survivor tells stories of Nazi pilots sneaking food to her and others as they were doing forced labor on German airplanes. She also tells of her boss at a potato chip plant where she was assigned another time providing her with medicine. She had just received a whipping of about 25 lashes for stealing vegetables, and was in terrible shape. He provided salve and allowed her to sit and rest at work as long as no other German came in. Other survivors have shared similar stories with me. Often, they say that if it wasn't for a particular German guard, they would not have survived. Then there are stories of those who are more famous.

<u>Major Claus von Stauffenberg</u>, a German soldier appalled by the atrocities committed by the SS (SchutzStaffel- Hitler's personal body guards), led a group of Germans who were opposed to Hitler and planned to overthrow him. After being promoted to General and Chief of Staff to a leading Nazi, Stauffenberg had access to meetings of high Nazi officials. He, along with others, came up with "The July Bomb Plot" in 1944, in which they planned to kill Adolf Hitler, Hermann Goering, and Heinrich Himmler. (The History Learning Site)

After six aborted attempts at taking Hitler's life, Stauffenberg placed a briefcase, which contained a bomb, under the table near Hitler at a briefing session. He left to take a pre-arranged phone call, and while gone, unbeknownst to him, an officer attending the meeting moved the brief case. The bomb went off killing four men, but none of them were the key officials targeted by the group. Stauffenberg was later executed by a firing squad, but his story lives on in the movie *Valkyrie.*

Was he a good German? Well, one could argue that. He did once support the Nazi party, join the German Military, and move up in its ranks, so perhaps he may not have been considered good, but at least, at some point, he demonstrated enough conscience to take great risks to stop Hitler.

Once Stauffenberg witnessed the heinous actions of the Nazis, particularly of the SS, instead of just attempting to get away from the party for his own sake, using plastic explosives, he tried to rid the world of Adolf Hitler and his highest ranking associates, sacrificing his own life in the process. Perhaps not always "good," He showed great courage, and he took drastic action at a time when many others did not.

StauffenbergPhoto: Public Domain

To many people, the name **Oskar Schindler** is already a familiar one. The Steven Spielberg movie, *Schindler's List*, poignantly recalls the story of one man's personal transformation as he comes to comes to terms with the plight of the Jews and becomes an important rescuer of many. Schindler was a hard-drinking, womanizing, member of the Nazi party.

At first, Schindler bought and built up an enamelware business, once owned by a Jew, and profited from the slave labor of workers from the Krakow Ghetto and Plaszow Concentration Camp in Poland. He fought to keep those workers from being transported to Auschwitz and created essential positions to assure he could keep them there and safe. Eventually, after witnessing the escalating violent and abusive treatment of the Jews, particularly at the hands of the commandant of the Plaszow camp, Ammon Goeth, he began to spend his own money to negotiate the release of his Jews. Ultimately, Schindler saved over 1000 Jewish people in this way along with all of their future generations. (Buelow, 2009-2011)

Oskar Schindler-Photo: Public Domain

Wilhelm Hosenfeld is probably best recognized for saving the life of Waldislaw Szpilman whose life story was told in the movie *The Pianist*. It was Hosenfeld who kept Szpilman's hiding location in Warsaw a secret, and supplied him with food, keeping him alive at the very end of World War II until the arrival of Soviet troops and the liberation of Warsaw from the German occupation.

Although prior to reading Adolf Hitler's memoir, *Mein Kampf*, he originally supported and joined the Nazi party, after reading it, he began journaling about the atrocities he witnessed. He ultimately became disgusted with the Nazi's treatment of the Jews. According to the Jewish Virtual Library, "In his writings, Hosenfeld expressed his mounting disgust with the regimes' oppression of Poles, the persecution of Polish clergy, the abuse of Jews, and, with the initiation of the "Final Solution", his horror at the extermination of the Jewish people." (JVL-Wilhelm Hosenfeld)

Szpilman was not the only Jew saved by Hosenfeld. There was also another, Leon Warm, who escaped from a train headed for Treblinka. Hosenfeld provided false identification papers for him and provided him with a job.

Wilhelm Hosenfeld (2 May 1895–
13 August 1952) Photo:Public Domain

Holocaust survivors would like you to realize that some of them owe their survival to a few good Germans. Not all of them were evil, and these survivors feel grateful that some had hearts and took risks to care for them.

Chapter Eleven

Survival

When thinking about the Holocaust, certainly the pictures come to mind of deplorable conditions, filth, waste, disease, starvation, and of course, cruel treatment and torture at the hands of guards and soldiers. Truly it is amazing that anyone survived at all. Ask ten survivors how they made it, and you will probably get ten completely different answers. The reasons why and methods for survival vary greatly from survivor to survivor. We will look at a few here that focus on survival both within and outside of the camp system.

Shamai Davidson in *Human Reciprocity Among the Jewish Prisoners in the Nazi Concentration Camps*, explains, "The Nazi concentration camp represents the most extreme situation for survival known to man." He continues by reminding us, "Furthermore, the motivation to continue with the struggle to live in the concentration camps was constantly and deliberately undermined by the ruthless system of unprecedented terrorization and dehumanization. (Davidson, 1984, pp. 555-572) How is it, then, that some survived when others could not? Were there some common traits in those who made it through the camps?

My friend Helen attributes her survival to a few factors. She does credit a few Germans for helping her in the camps such as bosses who brought her medicine or hid food for her to find. She also knows that without her sisters and brother who were in the camps with her, she may not have made it. Whenever one of them was ill or ready to give up the fight, such as during her long death march, the other siblings would pull the straggler along.

Thoughts of her mother kept her strong. Whenever she thought she might die, she thought of how her mother would cry and be so sad to lose her daughter, so she mustered up the strength to endure to spare her mother the sorrow. She had no way of knowing then, that the Nazis had already killed her parents and younger siblings.

Finally, Helen tells audiences that she lived to be the voice for those who didn't. As mentioned briefly in the introduction of this book, she particularly recalls the death march in which girls she had known all of her life would collapse and find themselves unable to get up. She is quick to demonstrate how the girls waved to those on their feet, and tried to call them back to get their help to get up. As they would lie there, too weak to stand, they would wave and call out. Helen wanted to go back, as did others, but the Nazi soldiers with their guns made sure that didn't happen. Had she or any of the other girls tried, they would have been shot.

That repeated scene has always stuck with Helen, and she mentions those girls whenever she speaks. If she didn't live to tell their stories, who would?

Similar stories have been told by other survivors. They attribute their survival to their support groups. These did not always consist of siblings or other family members. Often, friendships were formed that resulted in deep bonds and connections that were lifesaving. The Yad Vashem archives include the following explanation of just such a group of friends.

Ovadiah Baruch, a young Jewish prisoner who was deported to Auschwitz from Greece, notes that the support of his friends helped him survive. He states:

> During the death marches (from Auschwitz) we were three friends, Yom Tov Eli, Michael and I. We were connected heart and soul. Throughout the whole time we were prisoners in Auschwitz, we stayed in close contact…During the death marches, Michael developed dysentery. He was so weak that he could barely continue to walk, and he begged us to go on without him. Yom Tov Eli and I insisted that we would carry him and support him as best we could. (Yad Vahem)

caveswiki.wikispaces.com

Joy Lanys of Samari Communications shared her father's story with me. She says, "Hymie Itzkovitz beat the odds as a 9- year old boy who witnessed his father being shot and survived the Holocaust living in a subterranean environment. He recounted his experience for an article in the publication *Furniture Today.*

> "The first thing the Nazis did was to surround our town and create a ghetto. All the Jews in my village were herded into the center of town," Itzkovitz recalls. "My family did not comply and we hid in our house. My father was hiding near the chimney, but a neighbor spotted him and, fearing reprisal from the Nazis, gave him up. I watched the Nazis shoot my father on the spot." (Furniture Today, August 21, 2006)

After other hiding arrangements became too dangerous, Hymie found a remote area and dug an underground fortress. A farmer smuggled food to him and his brother, and in primitive conditions, they survived the war. (Furniture Today, August 21, 2006) Eventually, he immigrated to Canada and built a furniture empire with little to no education." What kept him alive? Lanys attributed it to "Drive, determination, and a passion for life."

Holocaust survivors want you to know that a strong desire to live can make all of the difference. Whether it be simply a yearning to see home again or a call to bear witness, when combined with traits such as Hymie's, "drive, determination and a passion for life," it can help you overcome anything, "even something as horrific as the Holocaust."

Many children survived only by the courage of their parents who sent them on a Kinder Transport or to live with Christian families. Both of these methods still involved great risk. Naturally, there was always the danger of getting caught, but more than that, and it is a risk that the parents took anyway, there was always the chance that the parents would never see their children again. Even if they did, there was every chance that the children would not remember their real names, their true religion, or even their parents.

Although in the famous *Diary of Anne Frank*, Ann's entire family stayed together in hiding, it was not a common situation. The Frank family, along with their guests, had a unique hiding situation, several rooms, and several people to provide for their needs, which enabled them to remain hidden for over two years. Most Jews were lucky to find space in a room for which they had to pay to share with several strangers.

In some cases, people survived on the run. They maneuvered through villages, farms, and forests, looking for food and shelter. Many had to use false identities. Some lived this way for years and ultimately survived.

Here, I will veer away from the direct survivor message theme of this book. Admittedly, this is a message that I would personally like to take the liberty of sharing with you after having spent so much time with survivors and deep in Holocaust reading and research.

Regardless of how these amazing and strong people survived, what methods they used, or what motivated them to keep going when they felt like giving up, the fact is that they made it through horrific experiences that many others did not, that many of us could not survive. For that, they deserve nothing less than our full respect, attention, and protection. Additionally, they deserve our efforts to share their stories and messages long after they are gone.

It is up to us to keep their stories alive by sharing them because if they are forgotten, the victims will have died in vain. The legacies of both victims and survivors go unheard, their voices forever silenced, and memories of them erased. Furthermore, we increase the danger of similar heinous actions in the future when we cease to raise awareness. We keep their stories alive and their voices heard when we share their experiences with our youth to assure that future generations will always know the truth, never forget, and never believe the deniers and revisionists.

Auschwitz- Photo Credit: Simon Bell

Chapter Twelve

Remember the Liberators

Imagine for just a moment that you have been ripped from your family. Maybe you have even witnessed the death of some of your siblings or parents. You have been locked up, beaten, starved, humiliated, sick, filthy, cold, and deprived of humanity. Suddenly, yet years later, help arrives. Although you may no longer look much like one, you are once again treated like a human being. The unfamiliar experiences of human touch and compassion return, and at long last, there is food. Of course, I did not personally live through this myself, but I can only imagine that the soldiers who arrived as rescuers would seem like angels, like finally, God answered the prayers and tears of millions, and sent deliverance.

The book *Dachau 29 April 1945 The Rainbow Liberations Memoirs*, is a compilation of various forms of eyewitness testimony in raw form of the liberation of Dachau. Memos, reports, and letters home written by soldiers and officers comprise this collection. In it is a statement that summarizes the effects of the liberation on these troops.

> For more than a half century, some Rainbow soldiers have been loath to talk or even think about Dachau. For them, that day, those hours, or perhaps just the few minutes they spent there were intensely personal and private. Dachau destroyed their peace. To dwell on it

> could make one lose all faith in our fellow human beings and abandon all hope for a better world. (Dann, 1998. p.x)

The book goes on to further express that some of these liberators were not even able to talk to their own wives and families of their experiences. Still others knew that they must. Some felt that April 29, 1945 was a day to celebrate the victory of life over death. That, along with the following date of the 30th are dates that I honor. On the morning of the 30th of April, the Rainbow soldiers went on to liberate my friend from Allach (the Dachau sub-camp).

Like other survivors and liberators, the time came when the members of the 42nd Infantry Rainbow division realized that they should tell of the horrendous sites that they experienced. Mainly they reached this realization as the result of increasing comments from revisionists, some saying there was no Dachau or that it was just a place for rehabilitation and rest. In the book, the liberators share:

> If these revisionists gain credibility, then we know the war is not over. The battle we must fight now is to preserve the memory of Dachau so that evil will be recognized and remembered. If we allow this memory to be destroyed, then evil will have triumphed. (Dann, 1998. P.xi)

I will not go into the specifics of the sites that these troops encountered in *Lest We Forget: Lessons from Survivors of the Holocaust*, because the intent of this book is not to focus on the death and deprivation or to dwell on the suffering, but rather to learn from the strength of the survivors who overcame all of it, but I will share just a few quotes from *Dachau 29 April 1945* so that you can see for yourself the impact that this group of liberators' discoveries had on them.

- Lieutenant Quentin F, Naumann said, "I… saw enough to be repulsed by the inhumane actions of the Germans." (Dann, 1998. P.136)

- Pfc Harry D. Gruel explained that, "The impact of what we had seen did not sink in until some time later." (Dann, 1998. P.136)

- Captain James B. McCahey stated, "That whole day at Dachau was a very difficult day and night to go through. I do not believe that the men involved, or I, will ever forget it. (Dann, 1998.p.137)

Just imagine what it must have been like for the allied troops who came upon the camps, and saw first-hand the conditions in which the inmates existed, and saw those prisoners who were barely clinging to life. Faced with the stark reality that the Nazis had committed such heinous acts for years, and seeing for themselves the astonishing number of dead and those left barely alive, liberators had to work through their own shock, disgust, and anger to save the remaining sick and starving survivors.

According to A Teacher's Guide to the Holocaust,

> The Allied troops were so outraged at what they found at concentration camps that they demanded German civilians directly confront the atrocities. U.S. troops led compulsory tours of

> concentration camps to the neighboring population. Some German citizens were forced to partake in the burial of countless corpses found in the camps. (The Florida Center for Instructional Technology, College of Education, University of South Florida, 2005)

Whether stumbled upon in the line of duty or as part of a compulsory tour, how does one ever get over that experience? Famous writer J.D. Salinger, a veteran and liberator, once said, "You never really get the smell of burning flesh out of your nostrils." (Shields & Salerno, 2013)

All of these years later, some Holocaust survivors, at least those who were liberated from the camps, remember vividly those first glimpses of their rescuers. In the case of my friend's liberation, she remembers a woman. Although at the brink of death, suffering from Typhus, she clearly remembers what she refers to as a "female soldier with bright red nail polish and lipstick." I have tried to find out who this woman was. I have been in contact with some of the liberators of her last camp, Allach, a sub-camp of Dachau, members of the 42nd Rainbow Infantry Division, mentioned above, but as of yet, I cannot figure out who she was. I believe she may have been part of a nursing corps, or the Red Cross, but I don't know for sure yet. What I do know is that this survivor at age 87 remembers her so clearly.

Most survivors remember their liberators, and we should not forget either. One Dachau survivor, Bill Lowenberg, who later became an American soldier himself, is quoted in *Dachau 29 April 1945* as saying, "There isn't a day that I don't thank the American soldiers who gave their lives and their energies to enable me to live with my wonderful family in the United States of America." (Dann, 1998. P. 211)

Although this book focuses primarily on Holocaust survivors, veterans have also been very important in my life. Not only do I come from a long line of veterans of just about every war in which the United States has been involved, but with my extensive Holocaust and World War II study, my appreciation for their experiences has grown exponentially. They too are leaving us far too quickly, and for that reason, I have also spent time getting to know Tuskegee Airmen and worked with Honor Flight, a wonderful program dedicated to flying these veterans to Washington D.C. to see their memorial while they still have the ability.

Just as I firmly believe that everyone should listen to survivors, I also recommend taking time to listen to the stories of veterans. Keep in mind though that as with the survivors, some will want to talk about their experiences, while others may not be able to, so approach it cautiously and sensitively.

Regardless of how old they get, the memories of the liberation do not fade. Holocaust survivors want you to know that they remember their "heroes" or "angels." They have not forgotten their liberators, nor should you ever forget the impact that these events had on their lives. They are a special group of people who deserve our respect and gratitude.

Young and old survivors in Dachau cheer approaching U.S. troops.

Chapter Thirteen

When Nothing Remains- Life in the DP Camps

When the Allied forces liberated the concentration and labor camps, in most cases, it was not as if the gates were flung open, and the inmates ran freely out to find happiness. Although in places such as Auschwitz, survivors were left to fend for themselves. For the most part, we must understand that there were several complicated factors involved. Liberation did not necessarily equate to freedom.

In *The Holocaust: A History of the Jews of Europe During the Second World War*, Martin Gilbert shares a story of a woman liberated by the Russians at Pruszcz. Sonia Reznik Rosenfeld described how the soldier told them that they were free and could go wherever they chose. She said that "Everyone lay motionless. No one could utter a word." She spoke to him, "I told the officer that we were half-dead people, and I asked him where we would go, and how we would get there as none of us had a home any more for Hitler's hordes had shot everyone's family." (Gilbert. 1985. p. 787)

The officer looked at them with pity and explained that they would be taken to their military hospital to convalesce before going on their way. He also assured them that one day they would be people again like others. (Gilbert, 1985 pp.786-787) This reassurance was great for those whose humanity and civil rights had been stripped away from them long ago. By the time of liberation, many surviving victims were near death. Either weak from starvation or ill with Typhus or various other diseases, they could not have all simply walked out if they had tried. Upon entering the camp of Bergen-Belsen, of Anne Frank fame, and the one that my friend describes as the worst of the seven in which she was held, soldiers were shocked. Without going into extensive detail here, I do wish to share just one observation so that you might glean a better understanding of the types of memories with which liberators must live.

Martin Gilbert states in his book that a British Army review reported, "Evidence of cannibalism was found. The inmates had lost all self-respect, were degraded morally to the level of beasts. Their clothes were in rags, teeming with lice, and both inside and outside the huts was an almost continuous carpet of dead bodies, human excreta, rags and filth." (Gilbert, 1985. p. 795) Certainly, such sites would have to affect liberators for the rest of their lives, but it demonstrates how they would have to set their own feelings and reactions aside because of the urgency of taking care of these survivors once everything had been taken from them.

Restoring their physical and mental health was necessary, and it was a costly learning process. After starving for as long as they had, certainly their first instinct was to eat to satiate their hunger, and naturally the liberating troops wanted nothing more than to feed and comfort them. Unfortunately, since the victims' digestive systems had all but shut down, eating foods to which they were no longer accustomed and so suddenly often resulted in death. Getting them back to eating normally was a slow process, and was done under the care and supervision of the American and British troops. Some eventually made it to hospitals and sanatoriums for recuperation. ("The liberation of Auschwitz -January 27, 1945", 2010)

Following physical recovery, the process began of piecing lives back together began. Remaining family members, what few there might have been, had to be located. With the help of The American Red Cross Holocaust Victims Tracing Center, such reunions were sometimes possible. Whether or not families could be salvaged, the question remained of where to go. Many of the home towns and villages of the survivors were destroyed during the fighting of World War II. Even those towns and villages left standing, had by this time been taken over by other people, often anti-Semitic former neighbors, who did not at all want to see the Jews return.

Conversely, many Jews did not wish to return to their homes filled with memories of now deceased loved ones, and surrounded by people who were so quick to turn against them, and who had so often assisted the Nazis in finding them. So where could they go? Soon, a name evolved for this group of victims/survivors. They were referred to as "displaced persons." Camps were set up to house them, some in recently liberated concentration camps such as Bergen-Belsen. Others were located in former SS barracks or abandoned apartments. (World War II - Rangers lead the way, 2013)

These camps provided food, shelter, health care, and educational opportunities as survivors looked for and awaited sponsorship to immigrate to other countries such as Palestine, the United States, and Canada. Spending several years in a displaced persons camp (DP camp) was not uncommon. Residency could consist of four years or more, following possibly several years of concentration camp incarceration.

This several-year disconnect from home and family does not even take into account those years lost to survivors during the German occupation of towns and villages prior to deportation. During those years, as mentioned earlier, Jews were restricted by the Nuremburg Laws, which kept them from public places such as theaters, stores, libraries, and school, to name just a few. Clearly, apart from the death of family members, and the loss of homes, the greatest travesty is that such a large portion of their lives were taken and can never be reclaimed. Although technically free during time spent in the DP camps, survivors were still deprived of normal life and family.

The Displaced Persons (DP) camps were established across Germany, Austria, and Italy to house the survivors left with no place to go after liberation. According to *the Holocaust Explained*, "At their height the DP camps held in excess of 250,000 Jewish survivors." (London Jewish Cultural Centre. 2011) Even in these camps, however, survivors still had to contend with shortages of food, unemployment, and housing that did not adequately meet their needs. (Sheehan, 2001. p.10)

Following years of psychological torment and being deprived of basic nourishment and necessities, returning to a normal life was difficult. Imagining a normal life was probably almost impossible for these camp residents because of the daily reminders of previous concentration and labor camps.

Housed in former military barracks, apartment complexes, and even former concentration camps, some were surrounded by fencing and armed guards, who in some cases, did not allow the residents out even to look for their family members. Holocaust survivors did not feel free. (Brenner, n.d.) A journalist commented that the mood of the camps was one of "apathy, grayness, and despair." Continuing on, the journalist described the people in the camp as appearing "demoralized beyond hope of rehabilitation." Additionally, to this writer, they appeared physically and spiritually broken without hope for the future. (Sheehan, 2001. p.10)

However, in the camps, there were often acting troupes, where performers could earn cigarettes and chocolate, precious commodities that could be bartered and traded. DP Camps also had sports clubs and training programs for languages and job skills. Schools were set up for the children. (Brenner, n.d.) Teachers arrived from the United States and Israel to educate the children of the DP camps. (United States Holocaust Memorial Museum)

As survivors of the camps waited to find new countries to take them and find sponsorship and the means to get there, they not only looked for remaining family and friends, but they also began to rebuild lives by forming new relationships. Many meaningful friendships developed, and love blossomed, in whatever form that now took, for people devoid of such sensibilities for so long. New families began to attempt to fill the void of those lost, and European Jewry began its rise from the ashes.

Religious schools opened in many camps, and with the assistance of Jewish volunteer agencies that supplied religious articles Jewish religious holidays began to take on a significant role in rebuilding lives of "normalcy." (United States Holocaust Memorial Museum)

Holocaust survivors want you to know that they were not suddenly freed at liberation to walk out of the gates and resume a normal life with friends and loved ones back home. Rebuilding took time and strength. No one should ever have to lose everything and be forced to start over with nothing because of the hatred and intolerance of others.

Chapter Fourteen

You can't go Home Again

Survivors of the Holocaust who had struggled to survive despite astronomical odds often did so by dreaming of one day returning to their homes and reclaiming what was left of their former lives. Even if they knew that they had lost family members, they yearned for anything familiar after the end of the war. Therefore, some did actually try to return to their homes as soon as they could.

Unfortunately, property rights seemed to mean nothing at all once all of the Jews disappeared from an area. At first Nazi soldiers, and later, former neighbors helped themselves to Jewish homes and/or their contents, benefitting greatly from the misfortune of their Jewish former neighbors.

My friend was not one of those survivors who wanted to rush back to their homeland. She had lost her parents, younger siblings, and other friends and family to the gas chambers of Treblinka. She knew there would be nothing left there for her, but eventually made the trip many years later only to share her Polish village with her daughters and grandchildren.

When she first returned to Poland in the 1990s, she was upset by what she saw. Her home had been destroyed, but so had the Jewish cemetery. Gravestones were shattered and used as part of the streets. As she tried to find familiar families, a former neighbor remarked to her guide that they had finally gotten rid of all of their Jews and chastised him for bringing them back.

She ended up returning again in the early 2000s. By that time, the village had been cleaned up, and the mayor, who had promised her years earlier, had stayed true to his word, and had the headstones removed from the road and rebuilt the Jewish Cemetery. This time, she and her family were treated better. She made one final trip in 2013 to attend the dedication of her former synagogue, which was renovated and turned into a Jewish cultural center. She does tell me that she will never again go back there, though.

When a former Auschwitz prisoner, Libusa Breder, returned to her town after three years in captivity, she went to the gate and knocked. A man asked what she wanted, and she explained that she had come back home. His response was, "Why don't you go back where you came from?" and slammed the door.

Libusa had clung to the dream of returning home throughout her time in the camp. After such a rude awakening on her arrival, she regretted ever having tried. She says that there was little evidence that Jews ever lived in the town at all, and "Everybody was keeping their distance ; it was as if I was poisonous. They probably were afraid that they would have to return confiscated property. I left the next day and never went back. To return home was my worst experience." (PBS and Reece, Auschwitz)

Thomas Blatt, a survivor of Sobibor, returned to his family home in the 1980s. The current resident allowed him inside, and Blatt immediately recognized his father's chair, and said as much. The man denied it, and claimed that he had purchased it. Blatt turned the chair over, and his family name was on the bottom of it. The man suddenly accused Blatt of coming there to find money that his family must have hidden. He even offered for Blatt to take the money out of its hiding spot, and they could split it. Instead, of arguing against the man's theory, Blatt just left. (PBS and Reece, Auschwitz)

Blatt did return again a few years later to find the home no longer livable. A neighbor explained that the man tore the house apart after the last visit looking for the hidden treasure that he thought was left behind. He could not afford to fix what he had destroyed and so he just abandoned the house, leaving it in ruins. (PBS and Reece, Auschwitz)

Returning home could also be dangerous for the Jews. After the war, in Poland, there were still pogroms, riots against the Jews. During one in Kielce, 42 Jews were murdered and many others beaten. (USHMM Aftermath of the Holocaust) "More than 1000 Jews were killed in Poland Between 1945-1947," and more than 100,000 fled left Eastern Europe. (Sheenan, 2001. p.11)

Martin Gilbert once pointed out that the Holocaust survivors did not expect anyone to understand even a small portion of what they had experienced, but they did expect to be left alone to live out the remainder of their lives in peace. Unfortunately, that was not going to happen. In addition to pogroms, there were random beatings and killings. No matter how governments tried to control it, anti-Semitism continued to run rampant. Nazi ideology had taken root and was still apparently widespread.

Possibly a destroyed Polish village- Unclear copyright- Public Domain.

Holocaust survivors want you to know that for many of them, returning home after the war was not an option. What the Nazis didn't destroy, former neighbors claimed, and ant-Semitism reigned. They were truly displaced persons.

Once travel to a new country became possible for the survivors either through sponsorship or relief missions, they had to relocate, settle in, and often learn a new language, sometimes while never knowing a single soul in their new locations. Often, they had limited skills as a result of losing opportunities for education thanks to Nazi rule. So where did they go and how did they get there?

According to the United States Memorial Holocaust Museum, with the establishment of the State of Israel in May 1948, Jewish displaced persons and refugees began streaming into the new sovereign state. Possibly as many as 170,000 Jewish displaced persons and refugees had immigrated to Israel by 1953. (USHMM- The Aftermath)

While many went to Israel, others immigrated to places such as Canada and the United States. After Congress passed a new immigration law in 1948, approximately 104,000 came to America, settling at first in New York and some in New Orleans and points west. (Powell, n.d)

Holocaust survivors want you to realize that not all former neighbors opened their arms to welcome them in after their ordeal and not all borders opened their gates to them. They struggled and waited for opportunities to find a fresh place to start their new lives.

Chapter Fifteen

The Terrors that Remain

Why it never occurred to me, I suppose I will never figure out, but a day came when a survivor friend and I went to visit a rabbi I know. Having known him for a while, I realized that in his disabled state that he was attended to by a service dog, one to which I had formed an instant attachment months prior. I took for granted that because this dog was such a kind and loving soul, that no one would ever fear him.

On a day when my friend was visiting, she requested that I take her to meet this rabbi. Excited to oblige, I made the arrangements, and we entered the rabbi's home. A look of panic swept over my friend's face, and it hit me at once, that the site of this dog made her uncomfortable.

Although she never spoke to me of having a fear of dogs, I was at once consumed with guilt for not having thought about or prepared her for this dog. How much of my normal life I take for granted! Why wouldn't she be uncomfortable at the sight of dogs? They controlled a great many years of her life, years in the concentration camps and for the years of the Nazi occupation of her town prior to her deportation. Early on in fact, she had witnessed a German shepherd at the hands of two Nazi officers attacking her father in the street, tearing his face to the point of bleeding. Of course dogs would intimidate her. Fear of dogs is not the only thing that I took for granted. I have learned in my association with these amazing people that there are many triggers for them, triggers caused by everyday occurrences you and I might never give a second thought to on our own.

A Totenkopf division SS member poses with two puppies in the Gross-Rosen concentration camp.

One such trigger is an ambulance or fire truck siren. Survivors have told me that every time they hear one, it is as if they are right back in the camps again. One explained that at each camp, there was a siren such as that to get the inmates up and out to roll call each morning. I couldn't help but remember this as I attended the opening of a Holocaust memorial where emergency vehicles passed by with sirens blaring during the outdoor ceremony. I wondered how many of the survivors there might be uncomfortable at those moments.

Roll call, also called Appell, always unpleasant, and often done in terribly harsh temperatures and weather conditions, could last for up to four, or five hours or more, depending on how long it took to get the head count right. Sometimes, there would be an additional nighttime roll call, usually used as a punishment. No wonder the siren would resonate with survivors so to this day. I now think of them each time I hear a siren. I think about how many times each day they must be haunted by sirens like these.

Members of the SS and police speak among themselves during a roll call at the Buchenwald concentration camp. (USHMM.org)

One other everyday item that is probably more obvious of a trigger is the sight of a train. After having traveled in jammed-packed cattle cars devoid of food, water, or anything at all resembling waste accommodations for days at a time, some survivors cannot ever ride a train again. On their deportation trips, many were packed into cattle cars with between 100-150 people to the point of being unable to move at all, much less rest or recline. Many people died as a result of being unable to endure the harsh travel conditions that somehow others survived. Every time they see trains, they are reminded of their transports.

In addition to trains, Holocaust survivors can also have strong reactions to particular car companies that relied on inmate labor during the Holocaust, such as BMW and Volkswagen. They must deal with these triggers every day as they see them on the road or pushed in commercials on television. We need to realize that things we take for granted, can actually still be quite traumatizing to them, and seeing or hearing these items is a constant reminder of their ordeal. Since the majority of us have never walked in their shoes, we have never come close to experiencing the atrocities that they lived, and we can never know for sure which events in our everyday lives might be a catalyst for painful memories or causes for fear for Holocaust survivors.

Photo Credit: Public Domain

In addition to their fears, survivors may have habits which may be difficult to understand, but if we step back and consider where these quirks may have developed, understanding becomes easier, as does tolerance when needed. One minor quirk is their reluctance to waste a scrap of food. In the case of some survivors, this is taken quite seriously.

One survivor, for instance may make herself a couple of slices of toast. If for whatever reason, she decides not to eat the second slice, she wraps it and puts it in the freezer for another time. I have always believed in preserving leftover food, but saving toast was a new concept for me. Yet, when I thought of her stories of how fighting for any small piece of bread in the camps, bread that was often, hard, moldy, or bug-ridden, became a way of life necessary for survival, I better understand. Considered in that light, it is easy to see how saving an entire fresh slice would be so vital to her.

I have noticed that other survivors share similar habits. I have heard of more than one saving every scrap of food. One might think that over time and in this time of convenient and fast food, that instinct would have lessened some, but apparently not. There are some who insist on sleeping with their purses at night, and still others who insist on multiple door locks.

Among other traits or habits, we might notice survivors over-protecting their children, secrecy, moodiness, nightmares, and other Post Traumatic Stress Disorder (PTSD) symptoms. Time does not seem to lessen these behaviors. As a matter of fact, recent studies indicate that these issues may intensify with age.

Anything might trigger memories for these survivors as they grow older. It might be a haircut, standing in line somewhere, a lack of privacy, or the sounds of crying or screaming that shifts them back in time. Any of these triggers contribute to the personality of the survivor which might affect everything from how they parent to how they age.

Holocaust survivors need you to remain sensitive to those habits that you don't understand, both their fears and their quirks, for the time we have remaining with them. Each and every one is founded in deep-seeded memories of a time in their lives that is foreign to the rest of us. We must remain cognizant of that and treat their idiosyncrasies with the utmost respect.

Chapter Sixteen

No one Asked

Surprisingly, many children of survivors never realized that their parents had any connections to the Holocaust. Of course, this was not always the case, but in my own Holocaust-related studies, I have encountered many stories of children who grew up without knowing until reaching an older age that their parent(s) suffered at such a deep level.

These second gens (for generations), as they are often referred to now, learned of their parents' involvement in various ways, but it seems that often, they opened up more to the third generation, their grandchildren. It is not unusual for grandparents to behave differently with their grandchildren than they did while raising their own sons and daughters. I don't think that is intentional. As parents, many had to work, but now they may be retired as grandparents. They may be more relaxed and have more time on their hands to dote on their grandchildren. Parenting is a skill that is also learned over time and through trial and error. A long time is needed to become comfortable with the parenting role. It only makes sense that by the time one becomes a grandparent, he or she is calmer and wiser.

However, these reasons do not seem to be the cause of the third gens being privileged to the information that the second gens were not privy to receive. A good example of this came to me from Josh Scharf, president of Archetype Ltd. whose father was a Holocaust survivor. He explains that his father, Israel Scharf, didn't talk about his experiences until he was much older. He would share the photos and mementos that had survived the war with his grand-daughters. Scharf explains that, "He shared more with my daughters because he knew that his time was short. He implored them to never follow the crowd and to always think for themselves." Israel's grand-daughters took those lessons to heart and they're both very accomplished and independent thinking young ladies.

Sometimes it is the realization that time is fleeting that makes survivors concede that they really should speak out and leave their legacies and lessons for future generations. Perhaps it happens because of other motivators such as increasing Holocaust denial or more interest and acceptance of the stories they have to share. However, when asked why they never talked about their experiences earlier with their own children or others as they were raising their families, the answer will often be, "They never asked." That answer strikes me every time I hear it.

Certainly there are others who could not discuss the event because of the traumatic memories and out of fear of opening old psychological wounds. I have met some of these silent survivors as well during the course of my studies, but the idea of not discussing their experiences simply because no one asked just amazes me.

Others might respond, "Who would have believed me?" I can't imagine the pain of holding in all of those memories, experiences, and sights out of fear that they would not be believed. Yes, clearly their experiences can be considered "unbelievable," but in order for us to glean any understanding at all, we have needed to hear about it directly from them. I'm sure that the words simply do not exist that can ever make any one of us truly know what they went through. No archived film, well-produced movie, or even first-hand account can ever accurately express the smells, the terror, the filth, the death, and especially the hunger associated with their harrowing experiences. It is just too "unbelievable," but at the same time, it DID happen, and we must learn about it from them and do our best to understand. We must believe even that which we can't imagine, or the chances become greater that it could happen again.

In the case of the third generation, the Holocaust has now been immortalized in books and film, and talk of it is no longer taboo. Survivors who feel more comfortable and secure may open up freely to their grandchildren on their own accord, but one key difference is that their grandchildren now ask.

Again, I will point out that many survivors did share their stories with their children. It may have even impacted their lives to the point that one would have to figure it out anyway. There doesn't seem to be a set pattern for the parenting style of those who survived and went on to have children. I have actually heard stories that are polar opposites. I have heard of those parents who were extremely sheltering and overprotective, and I have heard of those who were distant and could not form attachments and bond with their children after perhaps experiencing the loss of previous children in the camps.

Regardless of how survivors set aside those memories in order to begin a family (or a second family), it is to be commended. The second generation, third generation, and every subsequent one from here on, stand as a testament to the fact that Hitler did not win. He did not eradicate the entire "Jewish race," as he referred to it. Survivors have proven their strength and resiliency and in sharing those events of their lives prior, they can now pass on the truest history to help prevent it from ever happening in the future. We need not fear to ask the questions to do our part in the education of the next generations, but it is important to be prepared for varying reactions to those questions, and respect them accordingly.

Holocaust survivors want you to care enough to ask and find out the truth. Let them know that you will believe and pass on their stories and never take their experiences lightly. They want you to believe and never forget.

Chapter Seventeen

Research before you Vote

One must remember that Adolf Hitler did not fall into office by accident. While he was appointed as Chancellor first by President Hindenburg, there were elections involved. Daniel Lubin explains,

> Hitler came to power not through elections, but because Hindenburg and the circle around Hindenburg ultimately decided to appoint him chancellor in January 1933. This was the result of backroom dealing and power politics, not any kind of popular vote. It is true that after Hitler was already ensconced as chancellor, the Nazis subsequently **won** the March 1933 elections. But this was in the wake of the Reichstag fire, when the government had passed an emergency law that sharply restricted the activities of left-of-center parties (including the arrest of many Communist leaders).

Thus it is difficult to claim that these were "free and fair" elections.

According to the History Place,

On August 2, 1934, at 9 a.m., the long awaited death of 87 year old Hindenburg finally occurred. Within hours, Hitler and the Nazis announced the following law, dated as of August 1...

> "The Reich Government has enacted the following law which is hereby promulgated.

Section 1. The office of Reich President will be combined with that of Reich Chancellor. The existing authority of the Reich President will consequently be transferred to the Führer and Reich Chancellor, Adolf Hitler. He will select his deputy.

Section 2. This law is effective as of the time of the death of Reich President von Hindenburg."

These declarations were followed by a nationwide vote so that the German people could have the chance to show whether they approved or not. Hitler won approval with 90% of the vote (History Place, Hitler becomes Fuhrer).

The most frightening part of this is that his intentions were never a secret. While incarcerated in Landsberg jail for nine months in the early 1920s, he wrote an autobiography called *Mein Kampf* (My Struggle). In it, he makes no secret of his hatred of Jews or of his intentions for their removal. However, it must be noted that he may not have originally planned to murder all of them.

Early on, Hitler may have been satisfied with the removal of the Jews, and had they been accepted in more alternate locations, many additional lives might have been saved. However, there are some resources that show total annihilation may have always been the goal. Either way, his making the Jewish people into a scapegoat for all evils from the loss of World War I to the economic depression and high unemployment issues in Europe was clearly laid out and reiterated in *Mein Kampf*. (Adolf Hitler:

Excerpts) Regardless of those clear views, and his spelling out of the need to rid Europe of Jews, 90% of the German people chose to approve his role as Fuhrer.

I often wonder, how many people who approved of him even read his book. How many people checked out his background and history? How many people voted for him simply because he promised change? He promised jobs, healthcare, and a better tomorrow, and became a savior. Many, no doubt, casted their votes for him under pressure in an election that was not exactly fair, but votes in his favor were cast.

Researching a candidate before casting a vote is imperative. All politicians make promises, and while some are kept, how many are not? If we are going to trust our paychecks, our taxes, our retirement, our healthcare, our very way of life to a representative, shouldn't we at least look at voting records, written correspondence, and in our time, social media comments, just to name a few resources, to find out where that candidate stands on every single issue that matters to us?

Election line Photo credit: Annefrank.org

If we cast our votes based on slick television advertisements (remember Nazi propaganda), and do not research a candidate, we set ourselves up for disappointment at the very least. I am a firm advocate for exercising our right to vote, and everyone should, but only after researching the candidates before casting those votes.

In June of 2014, elections were held in Europe. In two different elections parties that are anti-Semitic gained seats. The fact that people, who in the aftermath of the Holocaust, should be fully aware of where such hatred and prejudice can lead can vote for anyone with anti-Semitic views just shocks me. Yet, not only did some vote in their favor, but enough did to where these seats were won.

During the summer of 2014, a Neo-Nazi group was permitted to form a political party in Argentina. Of course, Argentina is a place that has been notoriously pro-Nazi for a very long time. We can see this when we consider how many former Nazi officers found refuge there following World War II. These include, but are not limited to Joseph Mengele, Adolf Eichmann, and others. This knowledge does not make today's news any easier for me to digest. It makes me irate, and again I wonder sometimes if nothing at all was learned from what happened during the Hitler years.

Did people take the time to realize the views of these candidates before casting those votes? Did they carefully consider the future repercussions of supporting (even if done by their own silence) a Neo-Nazi group forming a political party? Could one of these acts end up leading to another Third Reich?

To prove the importance of such research, allow me to share a few of Hitler's early views with you, shared by of all people, Hitler himself. Please pay careful attention to the dates. Here are a few examples of Hitler's own words prior to the Holocaust.

Hitler's Conversation with Josef Hell, 1922

When Joseph Hell asked Hitler what he intended doing if he ever had full freedom of action against the Jews, his response was:

> If I am ever really in power, the destruction of the Jews will be my first and most important job. As soon as I have power, I shall have gallows after gallows erected, for example, in Munich on the Marienplatz-as many of them as traffic allows. Then the Jews will be hanged one after another, and they will stay hanging until they stink. They will stay hanging as long as hygienically possible. As soon as they are untied, then the next group will follow and that will continue until the last Jew in Munich is exterminated. Exactly the same procedure will be followed in other cities until Germany is cleansed of the last Jew! (Nizkor Einsatzgruppen, n.d.)

Speech delivered by Hitler in Salzburg, 7 or 8 August 1920. (NSDAP meeting)

> For us, this is not a problem you can turn a blind eye to-one to be solved by small concessions. For us, it is a problem of whether our nation can ever recover its health, whether the Jewish spirit can ever really be eradicated. Don't be misled into thinking you can fight a disease without killing the carrier, without destroying the bacillus.

Don't think you can fight racial tuberculosis without taking care to rid the nation of the carrier of that racial tuberculosis. This Jewish contamination will not subside, this poisoning of the nation will not end, until the carrier himself, the Jew, has been banished from our midst. (Speech met with Applause) (Speech delivered by, 1920)

Jackel, Hitler's Worldview, p. 52; from a speech at Nuremberg, January 13, 1923

The internal expurgation of the Jewish spirit is not possible in any platonic way. For the Jewish spirit is the product of the Jewish person. Unless we expel the Jewish people soon, they will have judaized our people within a very short time. (simpletoremember.com)

From Adolf Hitler (Mein Kampf)

"...the personification of the devil as the symbol of all evil assumes the living shape of the Jew." (*Adolf Hitler: Excerpts*)

In *Mein Kampf*, Hitler had written:

"If at the beginning of, or during, the war 12,000 or 15,000 of these Jewish corrupters of the people had been plunged into an asphyxiating gas...the sacrifice of millions of soldiers would not have been in vain." (*Adolf Hitler: Excerpts*)

Harriet Tarnor Wacks, Director, Holocaust Center, Boston North Inc, wrote. "The Holocaust should not be studied to terrify or to shock, either children or adults, but to teach what happens when a nation blindly follows a leader and conventional morality is abandoned." (1985) If we do not educate ourselves on the political positions of candidates, we do follow blindly, and it can result in serious circumstances. The importance of careful voting is seen in the acceptance of Hitler by the German people. According to The Learning Network (part of The New York Times),

> Hitler came to power through primarily democratic means, as the German public — devastated by economic ruin after the First World War — was receptive to a strong, nationalist ruler who could restore financial stability and national pride.

Regardless of your political affiliations, frustration with elected officials, or economic conditions, please remember the importance of researching your candidates and ballot issues before casting a vote to help prevent history from repeating itself.

Chapter Eighteen

Final Thoughts

I invite you to help me re-sensitize this generation and those of the future. In this age of violent movies and video games, perhaps our youth truly are becoming desensitized. The value of a human life seems lessened for some of them. When someone shoots, stabs, or bullies another to the point of instigating suicide, this is someone who does not value human life. That is the real issue here, and it is up to us to make others see this value, or better yet feel it. One of the best ways to do that is to listen to Holocaust survivors and encourage others to do the same. The emotional impact will be unforgettable.

Pictures are not enough. Seeing haunting images of liberated victims disturbs us, but it can honestly be hard for some to see those poor walking mere skeletons as human souls any longer. Their lifeless eyes devoid of spark, their emotions long ago stripped by unspeakable images and experiences left them as fragments of the people they once were. It is hard to visualize when looking at the photos or film footage, the lives they left behind, the vitality, the work, the play, and the relationships. Images cannot provide the missing human link, but their personal testimony can.

During one survivor presentation, as I touched a Star of David patch for the first time, I felt the energy, the despair, the fight, and it changed my life. I could almost feel the heart beating beneath the chest of which it was worn. Had I never met its owner that would have been powerful enough, but that it was shared with me by the person who survived a time when forced to wear it, made the impact of his story painfully real. Years later, I met another survivor who also carried his yellow star in his pocket, ready to take it out and share his stories at a moment's notice. The stories are there for the taking and most survivors willing to pass them along to you.

Additionally, I implore you to approach and listen to veterans. They too are witnesses who provide authentic first-hand testimony to the atrocities seen in any war situation, but in the case of the Holocaust, they can furnish much-needed proof in the fight against deniers. These witnesses can provide a unique perspective on the humanity and lack thereof of the survivors, moments after their discovery.

I have had some meaningful discussions as a result of noticing a veteran in a store or restaurant and striking up conversation. Often recognizable by the identifiable veterans' hats they wear, I always say hello and thank them for their service to our country. Before long, they begin sharing some experiences, and are usually open to receiving questions. It is also easy to see how much my appreciation means to them. The stories they share are a part of living history, just as those of the Holocaust survivors.

Experiences such as these will soon no longer be an option for any of us as these heroes end their time here with us. The yellow stars may remain, as will the written or recorded testimonies of those brave enough to relive their harrowing tales, but the human touch factor will be gone. Even after spending significant time with a survivor, we can never know exactly what he or she endured, but it is now the responsibility of each one of us to bring the passion to their stories, and continuously breathe life into each of their testimonies. If we don't do it, who will?

Elie Wiesel, famous Holocaust survivor, professor, and peace activist, once said, "When you listen to a witness, you become a witness." (Quote all, 2014) Listen to witnesses while the opportunity still exists, and then, I implore you, share with me in becoming the witness- lest we forget.

Afterword

There is so much more that I could have included in this book, so many more rescuers, liberators, acts of resistance. For that reason, this is not the only book that I will write on this subject. If you are a Holocaust survivor or close to one and have any additional messages that you would like for me to include in the next book, or would like to have your memoir written, please contact me.

Also, if you are a liberator, rescuer, or close to anyone with a significant role or experience with the Holocaust or World War II and feel that you could add relevant information or messages to this or future writing projects, I would love to hear from you.

Remember, your words can share history, change attitudes, and teach vital lessons for many generations to come. To add your voice, please contact me at D.CallahanWritingServices@gmail.com.

Debbie J. Callahan

References

References

Adolf Hitler: Excerpts from Mein Kampf.(n.d.). Retrieved from https://www.jewishvirtuallibrary.org/jsource/ Holocaust/kampf.html/12.htm

The American Experience.America and the Holocaust.People & Events | TheWarsaw Ghetto Uprising (April 19 - May 16, 1943) | PBS. (n.d.). Retrieved from http://www.pbs.org/wgbh/amex/ holocaust/ peopleevents/pandeAMEX103.html Rick Groleau (Producer), & Joseph Tovares (Director). (1994). *America Experience "America and the Holocaust"* [DVD]. Public Broadcast System.

Auschwitz-Birkenau History of a man-made Hell. (2005). *History of Auschwitz Birkenau.* Retrieved April 14, 2014, from http:// www.scrapbookpages.com/AuschwitzScrapbook/History/ Articles/DeathStatistics.html

Brenner, M. (n.d.). Displaced Persons After the Holocaust – My Jewish Learning. Retrieved May 10, 2014, from http://www.myjewishlearning.com/history/Modern_History/1914-1948/The_Holocaust/Aftermath/DP.shtml?p=1

Buelow, L. (2009-2011). Lest we Forget: Amon Goeth. Retrieved from http://www.oskarschindler.com/12.htm

Catcher, R. (n.d.). Stop Bullying Not Judging People Because of Their Race Religion Sexual Identity Or By Looks and Body Type Size. Retrieved May 17, 2014, from http://ryecatcher.hubpages.com /hub/Stop-Judging-Because-of-Race-Religion-Sexual-Identity-Choice-Or-Looks

Corrie ten Boom House Foundation, History.(n.d.). Retrieved from http://www.corrietenboom.com/history.htm

Dann, S. (1998). *Dachau 29 April 1945: The Rainbow liberation memoirs.* Lubbock, Tex: Texas Tech University Press.

David, A. (2014, April 27). Anti-Semitism On The Rise According To A New Report. The World Post [Tel Aviv]. Retrieved from http://http://www.huffingtonpost.com/2014/04/27/antisemitism-growing-euro_n_5221747.html

Denial: An Online Guide to Exposing and Combating Anti-Semitic Propaganda. Retrieved April 14, 2014, from http://archive. adl.org/ holocaust /denier_quotes. html#.U0xyLvldUpg

Dier, A. (2014, February 21). Japan mystery: Anne Frank's diary torn apart. Newser. Retrieved from http://www.newser.com/story/182688/japan-mystery-anne-franks-diary-torn-apart.html

Dvorin, T. (2014, May 18). New York: Black Cab Driver Banned for Wearing Swastika. Arutz Sheva Israel National News. Retrieved from http://http://www.israelnationalnews. com/News/News.aspx/180736#.U3iv2PRDtGg

The Einsatzgruppen Joseph Hell on Adolf Hitler. (n.d.). Retrieved April 10, 2014, from http://www.nizkor.org/ hweb/orgs/german/einsatzgruppen/esg/annihilation.html

Evidence from the Holocaust. In (2013). The Holocaust Encyclopedia.Washington DC: United States Holocaust Memorial Museum. Retrieved from http://www.ushmm.org/ wlc/en/article.php?ModuleId=100051318

The Florida Center for Instructional Technology, College of Education, University of South Florida (2005). Holocaust Timeline: Aftermath. Retrieved May 25, 2014, from http://fcit.usf.edu/holocaust/timeline/after.htm

Foxman, Abraham H., Anti-Defamation League National Commission Meeting New York, NY, November 1, 2007. Retrieved from http://www.adl.org/anti-semitism/united-states/c/anti-semitism-why-and-why-now.html on Mar. 16, 2014

Fromowitz, D. (2005, August 12). Importance of Document Retrieved from http://www.chgs.umn.edu/ museum/ exhibitions/rescuers/documents.html

German Voters Approve Hitler as Führer *By The Learning Network. The New York Times.* AUG. 19, 2011.HTTP://LEARNING.BLOGS. NYTIMES.COM/2011/08/19/AUG-19-1934-GERMAN-VOTERS-APPROVE-HITLER-AS-FUHRER/?_ PHP=TRUE&_TYPE=BLOGS&MODULE=SEARCH&MAB REWARD=RELBIAS%3AS&_R=0 Accessed Oct. 26, 2014.

Gilbert, Martin, (1985). *The Holocaust: The History of the Jews of Europe During the Second World War.* Henry Holt and Company. New York, NY. pp.786-787

Gilbert, Martin, (1993, May). Atlas of the Holocaust: the Victims of the Holocaust: an estimation...Retrieved from http://www.jewishgen.org/forgottencamps/general/victimsengl. html

Government of Canada, Citizenship and Immigration Canada. (2013). Backgrounder — working definition of Holocaust denial and distortion. Retrieved from website: http://www.cic.gc.ca/english/department/media/backgrounders /2013/2013-10-21b.asp.

"Hitler becomes Fuhrer," The History Place (1997). Retrieved from http://www.historyplace.com/worldwar2/holocaust/h-becomes.htm

History of Auschwitz Birkenau - Rudolf Hoess confession – death statistics. (2010, January 10). Retrieved January 1, 2014, from http://www.scrapbookpages.com/AuschwitzScrapbook/ History/Articles/DeathStatistics.html

History Channel (n.d.). *Warsaw Ghetto Uprising begins — History.com This Day in History — 4/19/1943.* Retrieved April 19, 2014, from http://www.history.com/this-day-in-history/warsaw- ghetto-uprising-begins

The History Learning Site: The July Bomb Plot.(n.d.).

Retrieved from http://www.historylearningsite.co.uk/july_bomb_plot.htm

The Holocaust: A learning site for students-Death Marches. (2013).The Holocaust Encyclopedia. Washington DC: United States Holocaust Memorial Museum. Retrieved from http://www.ushmm.org/outreach/en/article.php?ModuleId=10007734

The Holocaust Resource Center. Jerusalem : Yad Vashem: the Holocaust Martyrs' and Heroes' Remembrance Authority Retrieved from http://www.yadvashem.org/yv/en/holocaust/resource_center/the_holocaust.asp2.

Holocaust denial: An online guide to exposing and combating anti-Semitic propaganda. (2001).Estimated Number of Jews Killed in the Final Solution. New York: Anti-Defamation League. Retrieved from http://archive.adl.org/holocaust/response.html

Holocaust deniers and public misinformation.(2013). The Holocaust Encyclopedia. Washington DC: United States Holocaust Memorial Museum. Retrieved from http://holocaustroad.org/2010-11readings/Session13.pdf (2009).

Jewish partisans. In The Holocaust: A Learning Site for Students. Washington DC: United States Holocaust Memorial Museum. Retrieved from http://www.ushmm.org/outreach/en/article.php?ModuleId=10007743

Jewish Virtual Library Wilhem Hosenfeld retrieved from https://www.jewishvirtuallibrary.org/jsource/biography/Wilhelm_Hosenfeld.html on May 10, 2014

Klein, G. (2004, December 10). Transcript from an interview with Elie Wiesel. Retrieved from http://www.nobelprize.org/nobel_prizes/peace/laureates/1986/wiesel-interview-transcript.html

Kristallnacht: A nationwide pogrom, November 9–10, 1938. In

(2013). Holocaust Encyclopedia. Washington DC: United States Holocaust Memorial Museum. Retrieved from http://www.ushmm.org/wlc/en/article.php?ModuleId=10005201

Liberation of Nazi camps. In (2013). The Holocaust Encyclopedia. Washington DC: United States Holocaust Memorial Museum. Retrieved from http://www.ushmm.org/wlc/en/article.php?ModuleId=10005131

The Liberation of Auschwitz - January 27, 1945. (2010, January 4). Retrieved May 10, 2014, from AuschwitzScrapbook/History/Articles/Liberation.html

Lobe, Daniel, "No, Hitler Did Not Come to Power Democratically," The Lobe Log, Foreign Policy. (Feb. 2011). Retrieved from http://www.lobelog.com/no-hitler-did-not-come-to-power-democratically/

London Jewish Cultural Centre (2011). What were displaced persons camps? - Key Stage 3 - The Holocaust Explained. Retrieved May 10, 2014, from http://www.theholocaustexplained.org/ks3/survival-and-legacy/liberation-the-survivors/what-were-displaced-persons-camps/#.U245ZfRDtGi

Mongelli, L., Harshbarger, R., & Eustachewich , L. (2014, May 16). Swastika wearing taxi driver suspended | New York Post. Retrieved May 17, 2014, from http://nypost.com/2014/05/16/nazi-taxi-driver-who-wore-swastika-suspended/

Morse, S. P., & Lande`, P. (2008). Introduction to Dachau concentration camp records . Retrieved from http://stevemorse.org/dachau/intro.htm.

Myers, P. (2009, April 30). Pressac's proof in reply to Faurisson's challenge [Web log message]. Retrieved from http://mailstar.net/holocaust-debate11.html

Nizkor's The Einsatzgruppen *Joseph Hell on Adolf Hitler.* (n.d.).

Retrieved January 1, 2014, from www.nizkor.org/hweb/orgs/german/einsatzgruppen/esg/annihilation.html)

Pappas, Gregory (2014). Freedom or Death…On Holocaust Remembrance Day. Retrieved on Nov. 22, 2014. http://www.pappaspost.com/freedom-or-death-on-holocaust-remembrance-day/

Powell, L. N. (n.d.). The Holocaust and History: Introduction to the Survivors' Stories. Retrieved 25, 2014, from http://www.holocaustsurvivors.org/data.show.php?di=record&da=texts&ke=6

Public Broadcast System, & Laurence Rees (n.d.). Auschwitz: Inside the Nazi State . About . Transcripts | PBS [Video file]. Retrieved on May 17, 2014 from http://www.pbs.org/auschwitz/about/transcripts_6.html

Primo leader Itzkovitz overcomes long odds. (2006, August 21). Retrieved from http://www.furnituretoday.com/article/413172-primo-leader-itzkovitz-overcomes-long-odds Quote all the things. (2014, February 9). Retrieved from http://quoteallthethings.com/post/76120243105/elie-wiesel-quote-4447034

Representative Quotes from Holocaust Deniers. (2001). *Holocaust Rescue.*(2013). Holocaust Encyclopedia. Washington DC: United States Holocaust Memorial Museum. Retrieved from http://www.ushmm.org/wlc/en/article.php?ModuleId=10005185

Shachar Yigal, Oh Madre (Jerusalem: Yad Vashem, 2002), pp. 86-87, Hebrew]. Retreived May 17, 2014 from http://www.yadvashem.org/yv/en/education/educational_materials/adl/lesson5_community.asp

Shamai Davidson, "Human Reciprocity Among The Jewish Prisoners In The Nazi Concentration Camps", The Nazi Concentration Camps, Yad Vashem 1984, pp. 555-572.

Sheehan, Sean. (2001). After the Holocaust. Steck-Vaughn Company. Austin, Texas.

Shields, D., & Salerno, S. (2013, September 28). The life of J.D. Salinger: The stranger | The Economist. Retrieved June 9, 2014, from http://www.economist.com/news/books-and-arts/21586817-fascinating-unsubtle-look-complicated-man-stranger

Shofar FTP Archives:people/g/groening. oskar/press/guardian. 050110. (n.d.). Retrieved fromhttp://www.nizkor.org/ ftp.cgi/ people/g/groening.oskar/press/guardian.050110

Simpletoremember.com - judaism online: Hitler quotes.(n.d.). Retrieved from http://www.simpletoremember.com/ articles/a/hitler-quotes/

Sonderkommando. (n.d.). Retrieved June 13, 2014, from http:// www. themeadsofasphodel.com/img/Sonderkommando.pdf

Speech delivered by Hitler in Salzburg, 7 or 8 august 1920. (nsdap meeting) . *Hitler and Nazis, Statements Concerning Jews and Judaism*, Retrieved from http://users.ipfw. edu/bartky/Y200Y401 Judaism/Judaism Course-Hitler and Senior Nazis Statements on Jews.pdf

Study: Trauma of holocaust triples survivors' suicide risk. (2005, August 12). Retrieved from http://www.jweekly.com/ article/full/26747/study-trauma-of-holocaust-triples-survivors-suicide-risk/.

Tarnor Wacks, H. (1985). *HOLOCAUST CENTER BOSTON NORTH Why_Learn_About_the_Holocaust?* Retrieved June 12, 2014, from http://www.holocaustcenterbn.org/ why_learn_about _ the_holocaust.html

Teeboom, D. J. (2005, December 31).The Holocaust myth [Web log message]. Retrieved from http://www.think-israel.org/dec05bloged.html

Traubman, T. (2005, August 10). Study: Holocaust survivors 3 times more likely to attempt suicide. Haaretz. Retrieved from http://www.haaretz.com/news/study-holocaust-survivors-3-times-more-likely-to-attempt-suicide-1.166386.

UMKC (n.d.). Testimony of Rodolf Hoess in the Nuremberg Trial. Retrieved February 2014, from http://law2.umkc.edu/faculty/projects/ftrials/nuremberg/hoesstest.html

United States Holocaust Memorial Museum (n.d.). Displaced Persons. Retrieved May 10, 2014, from http://www.ushmm.org/wlc/en/article.php?ModuleId=10005462

United States Holocaust Memorial Museum (2013, June 10). Holocaust Encyclopedia Warsaw. Retrieved April 19, 2014, from http://www.ushmm.org/wlc/en/article.php? ModuleId=10005069

United States Holocaust Memorial Museum (n.d.). *United Nations Relief and Rehabilitation Administration.* Retrieved April 14, 2014, from http://www.ushmm.org/wlc/en/article.php?ModuleId=10005685

Victim of savage anti-Semitic attack in Paris recounts beating. (2014, March 27). Fox News. Retrieved from http://www.foxnews.com/world/2014/03/27/victim-savage-anti-semitic-attack-in-paris-recounts-beating/

The Village.(n.d.). Retrieved from http://www.auschwitz.dk/Trocme.htm

World War II: 42nd infantry "rainbow" division. (n.d.). Retrieved from http://www.jewishvirtuallibrary.org/jsource/ww2/rainbow.html

World War II - Rangers lead the way (2013, August 17). Displaced persons camp | World War II. Retrieved from http://www.desertwar.net/displaced-persons-camp.html

Wortman, Sciolino, Appelbaum *The Two-Thousand Year Road to the Holocaust.* "The Aftermath: The Debt of Memory and Survival is Passed Forward." Retreived on Nov. 21, 2014 from http://www.holocaustroad.org/2010-11readings/Session13.pdf

Photo credits

Death March from Dachau

Death March from Dachau- April 1945
United States Holocaust Memorial Museum Photo Archives
Courtesy of KZ Gedenkstaette Dachau
Copyright of United States Holocaust Memorial Museum, Washington, DC

Nuremberg

The defendants and their lawyers at the International Military Tribunal trial of war criminals at Nuremberg.
Photo Source: United States Holocaust Memorial Museum, courtesy of National Archives and Records Administration, College Park
Photograph # 61324
11/20/1945 - 10/01/1946
Locale:Nuremberg, [Bavaria] Germany
Copyright: Public Domain
Source Record ID: 111-SC-C-3700

Suicides

Photograph # 73886B
Caption: SS troops stand near the bodies of Jews who committed suicide by jumping from a fourth storey window rather than be captured during the suppression of the Warsaw ghetto uprising. The original German caption reads: "Bandits who jumped."
Date 04/22/1943
Locale Warsaw, Poland
Photo Source National Archives and Records Administration, College Park
Copyright: Public Domain
Order Photo #73886B Photo Credit:United States Holocaust Memorial Museum, courtesy of National Archives and Records Administration, College Park
Record Type Photograph

Danish Rescuers

Photograph # 70737
Caption: Danish fishermen (foreground) ferry a boatload of fugitives across a narrow sound to neutral Sweden.
Within just a few weeks of the first arrests by the Germans in 1943, some 7,000 Danish Jews managed to make their way to the safety of fishing boats that plied this route.
Date 1943
Locale Sweden
Designation RESCUE MISSIONS -- Diplomatic Rescue -- Denmark: Rescue of Danish Jewry -- Rescue Boats/Trip to Sweden
Photo Source: Frihedsmuseet
Copyright: Public Domain
Source Record ID: 12th Section
Record Type Photograph
Order Photo #70737

Dachau Liberation

Photograph # 45075
Caption Young and old survivors in Dachau cheer approaching U.S. troops.
Among those pictured are Juda Kukiela (middle), Tevya Grojs (second from the right), David Moszkowicz (fourth from the left), Szmulek Rozental (third from the left) and Gyorgy Laszlo Spiegel (second from the left).
Date 04/29/1945
Locale Dachau, [Bavaria] Germany
Photo Source National Archives and Records Administration, College Park
Copyright: Public Domain
Source Record ID: 208-AA-206K-19

www.ingramcontent.com/pod-product-compliance
Lightning Source LLC
LaVergne TN
LVHW051102080426
835508LV00019B/2026

9780692242841